ORCHID

Reaktion's Botanical series is the first of its kind, integrating horticultural and botanical writing with a broader account of the cultural and social impact of trees, plants and flowers.

ORCHID

Dan Torre

REAKTION BOOKS

Published by
REAKTION BOOKS LTD
Unit 32, Waterside
44–48 Wharf Road
London N1 7UX, UK
www.reaktionbooks.co.uk

First published 2023
Copyright © Dan Torre 2023

Printed and bound in India by Replika Press Pvt. Ltd

A catalogue record for this book is available from the British Library

ISBN 978 1 78914 708 7

Contents

Introduction

They are, surely, the most glamorous of plants.
— SIR DAVID ATTENBOROUGH[1]

Regardless of what you think about orchids, one thing that we probably could all agree on is that orchids are everywhere. They are ubiquitous. Go to virtually any supermarket and you will find masses of the plants. Visit any medical centre, corporate waiting room or hotel lobby and you will likely find a flowering orchid on prominent display.

Although orchids have always been popular as floral arrangements and as corsages, in recent years, orchid *plants* have noticeably impacted the cut flower industry. Instead of giving a bouquet of cut flowers, many will now opt to give a living orchid plant. It will likely cost about the same price, but the flowers will remain fresh, for months on end.

Orchids have the reputation for having beautiful flowers, with bright colours, delicate forms and beautiful fragrances. But they are also much more than this. Because of their huge numbers, vastly diverse appearances and expansive habitats, orchids have made an equally diverse and expansive cultural impact. Orchids are remarkably nebulous creatures. On the one hand, they can represent beauty, serenity and inspiration; on the other they appear deceptive, manipulative and nefarious. When we look deeper into the world of orchids, we will find that they are much more than an elegant flowering plant which resides, tastefully, on a receptionist's desk.

Oncidium papilio, from *Lindenia* (1887), vol. III.

Orchids are also everywhere in the natural world. They make up approximately 8 per cent of all the Earth's flowering plant species. There are roughly 28,000 species of orchid (and their numbers grow every year as new species are discovered). In fact, the orchid family is so numerous that simply providing a comprehensive listing of the full scientific name of each species would fill a book. Throw in the names of the over 100,000 recognized hybrids and it would make for a truly unwieldy volume.

Orchids grow virtually everywhere on Earth; remarkably, more than a dozen species are able to survive above the Arctic Circle.

Most orchids (about 70 per cent) grow as epiphytes – perched on the branches of trees in lush forests. The rest can be found growing in the ground as terrestrial orchids. A few species have taken the concept of 'growing in the ground' to the extreme, and live out their entire lives as subterranean plants, submerged entirely beneath the soil, even when they are in bloom.

Orchids are also shapeshifters. With so many varieties, many do not look at all as we would expect an orchid to look. Furthermore, many do not even look as we would expect a *flower* to look. Orchids seem to express an extremely capricious and malleable identity, both within the natural world and within our human imagination. Some can look quite strange to us – and often they can look very much like

Phalaenopsis cultivar.

9

something *else*. There are orchids that look like monkey faces, like flying ducks and some even remind us of our own anatomy. And importantly to many male insects, they can look so convincingly like a female insect that they will attempt to mate with them.

Orchids seem to be full of secrets and are willing to engage in some very unexpected behaviours. They are truly unconventional in how they interact with other creatures (especially their pollinators), how they develop, how they gather nutrients, and simply how they go about directing their lives – and seemingly, directing the lives of others.

Many of their structures and behaviours appear quite counter-intuitive – in some instances, it is surprising that they are able to survive at all, let alone thrive. For example, most other members of the plant kingdom produce nutrient-rich seeds, which ensure that they will germinate and have a good start in life. In contrast, orchids produce dust-like, nearly microscopic, seeds which lack all stores of energy and are entirely dependent on specialized fungi in order to germinate and develop. Most other plants that rely on insects for pollination will happily be pollinated by a wide range of resident

Brassada cultivar.

The monkey orchid (*Orchis simia*), a terrestrial orchid native to Europe.

creatures. However, many orchids will rely upon a single species of insect for pollination – and in some cases a single gender of a single species (for example, male wasps).

But ultimately, orchids have impact. As humans, we not only admire their unusual beauty, but we can readily identify with them. We can see ourselves in them, and we can appreciate (and perhaps be wary of) their manipulative ways. Philosophers have contemplated them, countless artists have celebrated them, billions of people have cultivated them, displayed them and even consumed them. They have occupied our thoughts, our stories, our societies, our greenhouses, our florists, our supermarkets and our homes. And that is merely the beginning.

Pl. 3.

LÆLIA MAJALIS.

Laelia majalis, from James Bateman, *The Orchidaceae of Mexico and Guatemala* (1837–43).

one

Understanding Orchids
ঽᙏ

T he Orchidaceae family is one of the largest of the angio-
sperms, and made up of over 28,000 species, which equates
to a sizeable portion (about 8 per cent) of all flowering
plant species on Earth. Simply put, there are *a lot* of orchids in the
world – and as would be expected, there is also a lot of diversity.
However, most orchids share a number of similar features, going
some way to unify this expansive and diverse family of plants.

Orchid Habitats

Orchids are generally divided into two broad groupings: those that
grow in the ground (terrestrials) and those that grow on other things,
such as trees (epiphytes) and rocks (lithophytes). About 70 per cent
of orchid species are epiphytic and are generally found in tropical or
subtropical areas with warm temperatures and high rainfall. Many
can be found growing high up in forest canopies. Importantly, epiphytic orchids are not parasites (as they were once believed to be),
but simply utilize tree branches as their perches. This lofty position
keeps the orchid away from ground-dwelling herbivores and the
deep shade of the forest floor, and brings them closer to sunshine
and fresh-air circulation. It also provides better access to pollinating
insects and birds and, importantly, facilitates the windblown dispersal of their numerous tiny seeds. Another advantage to living in
lush forest canopies is that there is continual falling organic debris

from both plants and animals, which can provide rich sources of nutrients.[1]

But this elevated habitat also comes with some significant drawbacks. Despite their lush tropical location, epiphytic orchids often experience almost desert-like conditions. They are exposed to periods of relentless sunshine as well as very irregular access to water and nutrients. As a result, many orchids have adapted some of the same survival strategies that cacti and succulents have. In fact, in Central and South America, orchids can actually be found growing alongside succulent epiphytic cacti (such as those belonging to the genera *Rhipsalis*, *Disocactus* and *Epiphyllum*). Appropriately, these cacti are often referred to as 'orchid cacti' since not only do they share habitats with orchids but many also produce large, showy flowers.

If we look closer, the similarities between cacti and epiphytic orchids are even greater. Cacti are well known for their succulent stems, which are capable of storing a great deal of moisture. Likewise,

Paphiopedilum spicerianum.

most epiphytic orchids have succulent parts. Many will have thick swollen stems known as pseudobulbs, which can store large amounts of water and energy. A number of orchids (such as the Australian *Dendrobium lichenastrum* and *D. cucumerinum*) also display thick succulent leaves, making them appear very similar to traditional succulent plants.

The unusual manner in which epiphytic orchids and cacti carry out photosynthesis is also similar; both are classified as CAM plants (which stands for crassulacean acid metabolism). For photosynthesis to occur, all plants must open their stomata (tiny openings in the epidermis) to let in carbon dioxide and release their waste product of oxygen. Most plants do this during the day when the sun is shining and they are actively photosynthesizing. However, when the stomata are open, a great deal of internal water can be lost to evaporation. Instead, CAM plants will close up their stomata during the day and open them again only at night, when it is cooler, thereby greatly reducing water loss. However, to cease 'breathing' during the day can present the plant with difficulties, as it needs to absorb carbon dioxide in order to conduct photosynthesis and expel waste oxygen. Since plants cannot conduct photosynthesis in the dark (the process relies on sunlight) the strategy is to absorb as much carbon dioxide as possible during the night, storing it as malic acid until morning. When the sun shines again, they use this carbon dioxide 'fuel' to carry out photosynthesis once more.[2] There are an estimated 30,000 species of CAM plants that can be found across the entire plant kingdom – remarkably, more than half of these belong to the orchid family.[3]

The roots of most epiphytic orchids are also succulent, and these thick whitish-green roots will sprawl out across tree trunks and branches and often dangle prominently in the air. They are covered with a unique coating called velamen, which acts just like a sponge and is extremely effective in absorbing water and nutrients. This allows the plant to very quickly (within a matter of seconds) absorb rainfall and water runoff. After absorbing moisture, they are very resistant to evaporation.[4]

Common button orchid (*Dendrobium lichenastrum*, syn. *Davejonesia lichenastrum*), an Australian orchid with noticeably succulent leaves.

Many epiphytic orchid roots will also carry out some level of photosynthesis. Although most epiphytic orchids are evergreens, some species, which live in particularly harsh and dry conditions, lose their leaves each year. Having lost their leaves, they can still continue to photosynthesize through their roots. A few species of orchids, most notably those belonging to the genus *Dendrophylax* (from *dendron*, a tree; and *phylax*, a defender), have decided that roots are all that they need and have virtually done away with leaves and stems. The most notable, *Dendrophylax lindenii*, also known as the ghost orchid, was popularized in Susan Orlean's novel *The Orchid Thief* (1998) and the film *Adaptation* (Spike Jonze, 2002). This species, when seen growing on a tree, displays just a mass of whitish-green roots. Only when it blooms does it look like an orchid, sending out large white 'ghostly' flowers, with long dangling nectar spurs, that seem to hover mysteriously in the air. Similarly, masses of thick green roots are all that is normally visible of the epiphytic orchid, *Taeniophyllum fasciola*. On the more diminutive side is the miniature leafless orchid, *Microcoelia gilpiniae* from Madagascar.

There are two main growth patterns found in epiphytic orchids, monopodial and sympodial. Monopodial orchids (meaning one foot) do not have pseudobulbs and tend to grow upright from one spot. The moth orchid (*Phalaenopsis*) as well as *Vanda* are popular examples of monopodial orchids. In contrast, sympodial orchids (meaning clusters of feet) have multiple pseudobulbs and these plants tend to grow laterally. During each growing season, they will push outwards, producing new adjacently positioned pseudobulbs, and thus adding to the overall volume of the plant. However, not all sympodial orchids produce conventional pseudobulbs (short swollen stems): some, such as many *Dendrobium* species (for example, *Dendrobium nobile*), produce tall, slender, cane-like stems instead.

Cucumber orchid (*Dendrobium cucumerinum*, syn. *Dockrillia cucumerina*), a succulent-leaved orchid.

Epiphytic orchids can also vary greatly in size, from the miniature (*Bulbophyllum minutissimum*, which reaches a height of only 1 centimetre) to the enormous (*Grammatophyllum speciosum,* which can grow to more than several metres in diameter). One specimen of *Grammatophyllum speciosum* was famously exhibited at the Crystal Palace in London in 1851. This massive orchid was said to have weighed nearly 2 tonnes.

Aerides houlletianum, from *Lindenia* (1887), vol. III. With its single (mono) central stem, it is an example of a monopodial epiphytic orchid.

Dendrobium strebloceras, from *Lindenia* (1887), vol. III. This orchid features long cane-like stems.

Terrestrial orchids typically grow in temperate regions, and can be found across much of Europe, Africa, West and Central Asia, North America and Australasia. Their habitats include grasslands and thinly wooded areas. Many terrestrial orchids are evergreen, but some are deciduous and will die back to their underground tubers during either the dry or cold seasons. As with their epiphytic relatives, most terrestrial orchids are adept at surviving periods of drought, storing moisture and energy (such as starchy polysaccharides) in their underground tubers. These underground tubers are actually the reason orchids are called orchids. The early Greeks decided that these tubers looked like testicles, and thus referred to them as *orkhis* (which means 'testicle' in Greek), and this eventually led to the family name of Orchidaceae and their common name of 'orchid'.

Orchis Robertiana.

Orchis de Robert.

P. Bessa pinx.

Barreis sculp

Indigène.
Fl. Mai. Juin.

1. Style et Anthère
grossie.
2. Pollen.

Terrestrial European orchid (*Orchis Robertiana*, syn. *Himantoglossum robertianum*),
showcasing its double tubers in a print from the 1800s.

Cymbidium cultivar.

Most orchids, with twin tubers, follow a growth pattern in which one of the tubers will provide nutrition for new growth, while the other will store up energy during the growing season. In this way, the tubers wax and wane from year to year. Some terrestrial orchids will also reproduce by sending out roots from their main tubers in order to produce daughter tubers. In this way, large colonies can emerge from a single plant. Of course, there are a vast variety of orchids, and their tubers also come in a wide variety of shapes and sizes. Some terrestrial orchids do not have any underground tubers at all; for example, most species in the genus *Cypripedium* will instead develop thick masses of roots.

There are a few species that are considered to be both terrestrials and epiphytes, and are sometimes referred to as hemiepiphytic. For example, the vanilla orchid begins life as a terrestrial, and then will seek to climb up the trunk of a tree; it will eventually divest itself of its terrestrial roots, and exist purely as an epiphyte on the tree branches.

Orchid Flowers

An orchid's flower spike, or inflorescence, can vary greatly in size and in the number of flowers it displays. Some species will produce just a single flower at the end of the spike (for example, slipper orchids), while others may have hundreds of smaller flowers in an effervescent 'spray'. But others will simply produce very small flowers that are tucked among equally small leaves. Some, such as those in the genus *Pleurothallis*, may produce a single tiny flower carefully placed atop the flat surface of a small oval-shaped leaf. Flower sizes can also vary greatly; some orchids produce flowers which measure less than a millimetre across, while others such as *Cattleya warscewiczii* can be 20 centimetres (8 in.) or more across.

STANHOPEA TIGRINA.

Stanhopea tigrina, from James Bateman, *The Orchidaceae of Mexico and Guatemala* (1837–43).

Dendrobium hybrid.

Orchids have the reputation for having long-lasting flowers; but this can also vary substantially. The flowers of the ubiquitous *Phalaenopsis* hybrids, the moth orchids that we are all familiar with, will normally last a few months. The flowers of *Dendrobium cuthbertsonii* are considered to be one of the longest-lasting flowers of the orchid family, persisting for up to six months or more. It is suggested that one of the reasons that orchids have such enduring flowers is that it gives them a better chance at pollination, as they wait patiently for their exclusive pollinator to do its job.[5] However, on the other end of the scale, some orchid flowers will only last a day or two (such as *Stanhopea* species), while the flowers of the vanilla orchid will last only a few hours.

Most flowers in the plant kingdom have radial symmetry: they tend to be circular in shape and have evenly arranged petals and sepals. If you were to bisect them – in any direction across their face – you would end up with two essentially identical halves. Roses, geraniums (and the flower heads of daisies and sunflowers) are all prominent examples of radial symmetry. In contrast, orchid flowers have bilateral symmetry: they have only one plane of symmetry and can only be

The white egret orchid (*Pecteilis radiata*, syn. *Habenaria radiata*).

divided evenly in one direction (vertically). This is also known as mirror symmetry (or being zygomorphic). Since orchids are not constrained to a simple round form, they have a lot more potential for variation, not only making them more fascinating to us humans but allowing them to better attract and engage with very specific pollinators. There are other flowers in the plant kingdom that also have bilateral symmetry (for example, snapdragons), but orchids arguably use this design structure to its fullest potential.

Bilateral symmetry also gives the orchid flower an orientation and thus we can easily talk about how the left side of the flower is identical to the right side (and how the top half is not identical to

the bottom half). Because of this symmetrically induced directional-
ity, we can also recognize that most orchids are technically upside
down (resupinate). That is, when the orchid flower is developing
(and still in its bud form), it will slowly rotate 180 degrees, situating
the labellum (a modified petal), which would have been its topmost
petal, as its lowermost petal. This resupinate orientation also allows
the flowers to make better use of their labella when they engage with

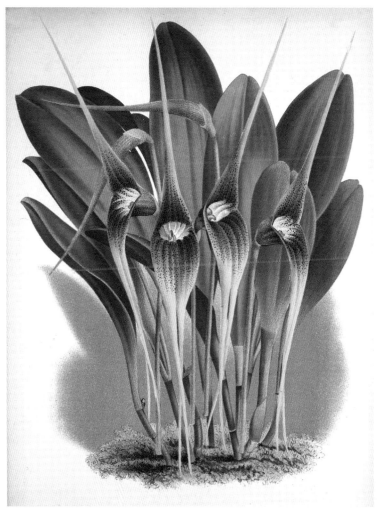

Masdevallia macrura, from *Lindenia* (1887), vol. III.

their pollinators (for example, to work as a landing pad or as a liquid-filled pouch). A few orchids do not rotate at all and are called non-resupinate, however, at least one orchid species (*Angraecum superbum*) will actually rotate a full 360 degrees so that, although it rotates during development, it ends up being a non-resupinate flower.[6] However, this upside-down orientation is not to be confused with certain orchid varieties, such as the epiphytic *Stanhopea* orchids, which are sometimes called 'upside-down orchids' because their flowers will dangle down below the base of the plant.

In addition to their bilateral symmetry, orchid flowers share a number of common features which make most easy to identify as 'orchids'. However, it is best to think of this structure (as with their symmetrical formation) as merely a set of guidelines – since the actual *appearance* of an orchid flower can vary immensely from species to species.

Fundamentally, orchid flowers have six petal-like parts (perianth), consisting of three sepals, two regular petals, and a third highly modified petal known as the lip or labellum. The sepals serve as the outer enclosure when the flower is in bud; but when the flower opens, the three sepals are normally spaced, alternatingly, between each of the three petals. (However, in some cases, the sepals may be fused together into what is referred to as a synsepalum.[7]) The two regular petals normally protrude from each side of the flower. These two identical petals can express a wide range of forms, including simple rounded shapes protruding like small wings, or, as in the slipper orchid, *Phragmipedium warszewiczianum*, they may be expressed as very long, thin dangling 'ribbons'. The third petal, known as the labellum, protrudes from the flower's centre and is often elaborately showy. It may appear as a large protruding platform, a deep tunnel or, in the case of the slipper orchid, as a large pouch. A primary function of the labellum is to attract pollinators and to act as a landing platform. However, because of its specialized design, some have noted that it also 'functions as a selector of pollinators' because it is also very effective at *discouraging* unwanted insects.[8]

Cattleya wallisii (left), *Calochilus platychilus* (right). Although orchid flowers can vary enormously in appearance, they all tend to have a similar structure, comprising six 'petal' parts: a) two regular petals; b) one labellum; c) one dorsal sepal; and d) two lateral sepals. Orchid flowers also have identical left and right sides, known as bilateral symmetry (or mirror symmetry).

Another highly developed feature of nearly all orchid flowers is that their male and female sexual parts are fused together into a single structure (referred to simply as the column). In this way, the two gendered parts are mostly inaccessible to each other, which greatly diminishes the chances of self pollination (which would reduce genetic diversity).

Additionally, instead of producing powdery dust-like grains of pollen (as nearly all other flowers do), orchids produce sticky masses, called pollinia. A single one of these can contain many thousands (or even hundreds of thousands) of grains of pollen. The sticky globs of pollinia help to prevent the pollen from being eaten by scavenging insects, being blown away in the wind or prematurely falling off their pollinating insect. Most importantly, they also help to facilitate a very focused strategy of pollination, as they ensure that a sizeable amount of pollen will be delivered to the next orchid flower in a single transfer. Often, the pollinia will be elevated upon a thin stalk called a stipe, which has a sticky base called a viscidium (this overall structure is known as the pollinarium). Normally, each flower will produce two

Orchid cultivar.

pollinia (but sometimes they will make four, six or eight). One notable exception can be found in the flowers of the widely cultivated vanilla orchid (*Vanilla planifolia*). Instead of pollinia, these orchid flowers produce conventional powdery grains of pollen.

Orchids, more than any other group of plants, seem to have the most directed and elaborate relationships with their pollinators. This is particularly true of how they attract their pollinators. Often an orchid will use clearly deceptive means to lure an insect and then to compel them to transport their pollinia to the next flower. For example, an orchid may only 'pretend' to offer nectar, or it may mimic another species of flower, or even a female insect.

Most non-orchid plants will, from the outset, produce fully developed flowers, which will also contain fully developed egg cells (ovules). After the flower has been pollinated, seed development will commence quickly. However, orchids will wait until their flowers have actually been pollinated before their ovule fully develop. This makes sense, as many orchid flowers fail to be pollinated, and by delaying ovule development they also avoid wasting resources. Once the pollinia have been deposited on the orchid flower's stigma, an auxin (plant hormone) is released by the pollen which stimulates the development of the flower's embryo sac.[9] Ovule maturity then follows, and microscopic pollen tubes will germinate from the pollinia and grow down through the column to fertilize these egg cells.[10] Eventually, mature orchid seeds will form. Because of the orchid's delay in ovule development, seed production will also be significantly delayed. For example, in the orchid species *Acampe reinschiana*, it can take more than sixteen months from the time of initial pollination through to seed maturation.[11]

From Seed to Seedling

Orchid seeds are extremely small (most look like very fine dust or powder) and, in fact, are considered to be the smallest seeds of any flowering plant. These tiny seeds are produced in a fruit, although because it will quickly dry out, it is frequently referred to as a capsule. These capsules can range greatly in size and shape and vary in the number of seeds that they contain. The capsule of some species will contain just a few hundred seeds, while the capsules of *Cymbidium tracyanum* can contain up to 3 million seeds.[12] The most abundant seed capsules are produced by *Cycnoches ventricosum*, which are estimated to hold more than 4 million seeds per capsule (totalling as many as 74 million seeds per plant).[13]

The reason why orchid seeds are so small is that they do not contain any stores of energy or nutrients. They are made up simply of an embryo and a very thin seed coating (known as the testa). Most will also contain a relatively large pocket of air, which makes up about half of the seed's volume.[14] Therefore, each individual seed is very 'inexpensive' to produce; however, as so many are produced, the total

Variety of orchid seed capsules.

expenditure is probably similar to that of non-orchid plants that produce far fewer, but better resourced, seeds.[15] When the seeds are mature, the seed capsules will split open, releasing the orchid seeds to the wind. These incredibly small and lightweight seeds will be distributed widely, drifting freely on the slightest air currents.

Despite their vast numbers, most orchid seeds will never germinate. Because orchid seeds lack energy stores, they must rely upon

A variety of orchid seeds, greatly magnified. Most are
so small they appear as specks of dust to the naked eye.

specialized fungi to provide them with the necessary energy, nutrients
and hormones. An orchid seed must become infused with a specific
species of mycorrhizal fungi in order to germinate. Orchid seeds, it
seems, lack not only stores of nutrition but the 'metabolic machinery
required for the utilization of the starch and lipids' (and are reliant
upon the mycorrhizal fungi for this functionality as well).[16] That
an orchid seed will meet up with a compatible fungus is far from

guaranteed, which is a significant reason why orchids produce such large quantities of seeds. At the end of the nineteenth century, Charles Darwin noted that 'if their seed or seedlings were not largely destroyed, any one [orchid species] would immediately cover the whole land.'

Simply releasing millions of ineffectual seeds to the wind may seem like a rather reckless approach, but the orchid does have an underlying strategy. First, there is success in numbers. Even if just one-hundredth of 1 per cent (0.01 per cent) of a flower's seeds germinate, hundreds of seedlings will still result. Additionally, the wind dispersal of tiny, balloon-like seeds encourages a very wide distribution, and further encourages epiphytic seeds to reach high into the treetops. Although most seeds will not come into contact with compatible fungi, those that are able to are virtually guaranteed successful development. In this way, an orchid's seemingly chaotic and random seed dispersal will, nevertheless, eventuate into a controlled and successful outcome.

The seed germination process of an orchid is entirely different to that of other plants. First, in order to begin the germination process,

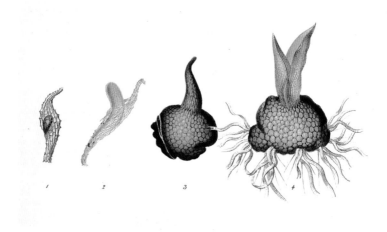

The development from orchid seed to protocorm (a life stage unique to the orchid family): 1) orchid seed; 2) embryo infused with mycorrhizal fungi bursts out of its seed coating (testa); 3) young protocorm, with an early leaf emerging from top; and 4) hair-like roots emerge from base of protocorm. Eventually a mature root and mature leaf will emerge.

Dendrochilum tenellum has fine grass-like leaves. It is commonly referred to as a necklace or chain orchid, due to its delicate chains of flowers.

it must attract and then be infused with an appropriate species of mycorrhizal fungi. Once this has occurred, the embryo of the seed will swell up and burst out of its testa. The orchid embryo will then transform into what is called a protocorm, which is essentially a little green ball of cells. If orchids were insects, we might think of this stage as their larval (or nymph) stage. Both epiphytic and terrestrial orchids go through the protocorm stage. As this little ball of green cells continues to grow, the protocorm will eventually sprout tiny rhizoid (or root-like) hairs at its base. Although significantly larger than a seed, a protocorm, at this stage of development, will rarely be more than 1 millimetre across. Depending on conditions, the orchid may remain in this protocorm state for months, or even years. As the protocorm matures, an early form of a leaf will emerge from the top and an early root will emerge from the base. Eventually both the leaf and root will mature and the orchid will become a seedling.

As we learn more about each species of orchid, we are also learning more about the specific fungi associated with each species. For example, the underground orchid, *Gastrodia elata*, is normally associated with the fungus *Armillaria mellea*.[18] However, the relationship that

Epidendrum ibaguense, sometimes referred to as the crucifix orchid.

orchids have with their mycorrhizal fungi can be fluid and the orchid may switch to other species of fungi as the plant matures. Terrestrial orchids appear to be more dependent on fungi throughout their lives than epiphytic orchids.[19]

Scientists now believe that orchids first grew over 100 million years ago in Australia (which at the time was part of the supercontinent Gondwana) and subsequently spread across the globe.[20] This would suggest that orchids existed alongside dinosaurs. Of course, having very meagre fossil records does make their evolutionary history somewhat obscure. But a remarkable discovery was made in 2005 when an extinct bee was found encased in amber in the Dominican Republic. The extinct bee and amber casing was dated as being 15–20 million years old. Even more remarkable was the fact that there were orchid pollinia attached to the back of the insect. The orchid to which the pollinia belonged was posthumously named *Mellorchis caribea*.[21] Undeniably, orchid flowers exhibit a great deal of complexity and specialization, which also seems to suggest their early establishment in plant evolution.[22]

two
The Secret Life of Orchids
❧

On the face of it, we might think of orchids simply as plants that produce beautiful, albeit slightly unusual, flowers. However, hidden behind this aesthetic facade, orchids engage in some very remarkable and extremely complex clandestine behaviours. On reflection, we might even begin to imagine that they are involved in some sort of elaborate, orchid-choreographed, performance.

Orchid Choreographies

Orchid flower pollination can be an enormously complex event. It normally involves attracting insects through the use of highly targeted visual and chemical signals. Upon arriving at a flower, the insect will be laden with pollinia. The situating of the pollinia is usually a very precise affair. The orchid flower will need to guide the insect into position in a very exact manner, often with a required accuracy of just 1 millimetre – and sometimes even less.[1] For example, the orchid *Habenaria obtusata* (syn. *Platanthera obtusata*) must be able to accurately place its pollinia directly onto the eyeball of a tiny mosquito! In many instances, the attached pollinia will begin to dry, and in doing so, will slowly change orientation (from, for example, an upright vertical stance to a horizontal one). Upon reaching a second flower, the insect will

Bulbophyllum grandiflorum, from *Lindenia* (1887), vol. III.

again be guided into a very precise position, where it will unwittingly deliver the pollinia (dried and therefore at an adjusted angle) onto the flower's receptive stigma.

The ideal surfaces for affixing pollinia tend to be the smoothest parts of the pollinator – in many cases this will be the insect's eyeballs, mouth parts or a specific area of its back (or in the case of a humming-bird, its smooth beak).[2] This is in stark contrast to the methods used by most other flowers, which produce powdery pollen. These flowers can afford to simply, and haphazardly, dust their pollen all over the insect's fluffy hairs and uneven surfaces, where it is sure to cling.

Most orchids make use of their bilateral symmetry in order to ensure that their insect pollinator is in a proper vertical position-ing. In this way, the orchid is able to place its two pollinia squarely onto the insect – for example, one on each eyeball. Thus, many orchid

A moth with orchid pollinia stuck to both of its eyeballs. William H. Gibson illustrates the drying process of attached pollinia in his book *My Studio Neighbors* (1898). Over time, the pollinia will droop forward from the upright position of 'C' to the forward pointing position of 'D', so as to be in the correct orientation to make contact with the next visited flower's stigma. Insect eyeballs are ideal smooth surfaces for pollinia to adhere to.

Cymbidium cultivar.

flowers will entrust an insect to carry their entire supply of pollen in one go. However, a few orchids seem to have developed another strategy. The crane fly orchid (*Tipularia discolor*), for example, is one of the very few orchids that do not exhibit perfect bilateral symmetry. It is more accurately described as having a modified form of bilateral symmetry, or perhaps even edging towards an asymmetrical structure. The crane fly orchid's flowers are pollinated by a moth (*Pseudaletia unipuncta*), which uses its long proboscis to drink from the flower's nectar spur. Since the alignment of the flower's petals and column is slightly skewed sideways, the moth's head is coaxed into not being precisely perpendicular to the flower. With its head tilted slightly to one side, the pollinia can only be attached to just *one* of the moth's eyeballs. A similar strategy seems to be employed in the South African orchid species *Bonatea speciosa*. This orchid has a small projection in the centre of the entrance to the flower's nectar spur. This forces the moth to tilt its head, either to the left or to the right, when it drinks the nectar. Thus, it too receives just one of the pollinia, which is attached to just one eyeball.[3]

There is a large grouping of tropical orchids (some seven hundred species) that are exclusively pollinated by euglossine bees; they are thus referred to as the 'androeuglossophilous' flowers.[4] The euglossine bees engage in a very complex courtship ritual, where the male bee will collect a range of floral fragrances that he will mix together in order to produce a unique female-attracting pheromone. These much sought-after fragrances are usually produced by the orchid flowers in the form of oils or waxy substances and the bees will collect these, normally adhering them to their hind legs. In some cases, the bee will secrete a fatty substance which aids in collecting the flower's scent. Because of the elaborate nature of this scent-collecting process, the bees are compelled to visit a large number of flowers (and therefore are very effective at cross-pollinating). However, it is an extremely arduous and time-consuming endeavour for the bees; and if one happens to come across a dead male bee of the same species, he will not hesitate to steal the fragrances from the legs of the bee corpse.[5]

Orchid Deception

Nearly all flowers that rely upon pollinators will engage in some form of deceptive behaviour. Their pollinators are essentially hoodwinked into carrying pollen, from one flower to another. Although the flower will usually offer the visiting creatures nectar, which they will happily consume, they do not necessarily consent to transporting the flower's pollen; or for that matter, assisting in the flower's sexual reproduction. From our humble human perspective, it seems like a harmless enough arrangement and one that does not seem to overly inconvenience the insect. In the case of orchids, though, things can appear to be much less equitable. Although many orchids do offer standard nectar rewards, many others will resort to flagrant deception. Their widespread, widely documented and seemingly advanced methods of choreographed trickery and deceit are unparalleled in the plant kingdom.

There are some advantages to engaging in pollinator deception. One obvious benefit is that, by not making nectar, the orchid will save a lot of resources (nectar can be very 'expensive' to produce). However, most surprisingly, the use of deception can also help to ensure 'high pollinator fidelity due to the specificity of the interaction' and,

Catasetum bungerothi, from *Lindenia* (1887), vol. III.

often, 'increased probability of outcrossing'.[6] Studies have found that when a flower *does* provide a nectar reward, the pollinating insect will (after drinking the nectar) tend to move on to the next closest flower. Although convenient for the insect, this means that the flower will probably receive pollen from a flower of the same plant (self-crossing).[7] Yet, if an insect visits a flower that purports to offer nectar, but it does not find any, it will, perhaps out of frustration, travel further afield before trying again.

But once an insect has been fooled, it might be more difficult to fool them again. To help counter this, each individual plant of some food-deceptive orchid species will express slight variations in fragrance. It is believed that this helps to ensure that the insect will continually be fooled, as it travels from plant to plant.[8] It is in the orchid's best interest to coerce its pollinators into visiting entirely different plants. Studies have shown that orchids that have been out-crossed will not only pass on greater genetic diversity, they will frequently produce more viable seeds than self-crossed plants.[9]

There are a wide range of tactics that orchids employ in order to deceive their pollinators (and it seems that more methods are being discovered all the time). These strategies of deception can include food deception, enemy deception, shelter deception, brood-site deception and sexual deception.

Food deception

Food deception is one of the most common methods of deception, and it is estimated that about one-third of all orchid species are food-deceptive.[10] There are a number of ways that orchids will falsely advertise that they are offering nectar, including flower colouring, fragrance, the presence of nectar spurs (though empty), and special patterns or growths which serve as 'nectar guides' (that misleadingly point towards where the nectar *would* be). Some orchids will also mimic (primarily through adaptations of colouring and scent) nearby non-orchid flower populations which *do* offer nectar rewards. In these

Blowflies pollinating a cluster of flowers of the orchid *Bulbophyllum lasianthum.*

instances, their resemblance will appear so similar that the pollinating insects will be unable to distinguish between the different species.[11] Curiously, many of the orchid species found in the *Vanilla* genus are food-deceptive, which seems rather ironic given the fact that the 'fruit' of *Vanilla planifolia* produce one of the most commonly consumed food flavourings in the world.

Nectar is not the only food that orchids might pretend to offer their pollinators. For example, the orchid *Bulbophyllum phalaenopsis* showcases coloured hairs (and fetid odours), which suggest to their pollinators the presence of maggots – which just so happen to be their favourite food.[12] Other orchids, by their scent and appearance, will promise carrion or other rotting foods, which will attract pollinating blowflies hoping for a meal.

Prey deception

Another more elaborate version of food deception falls under the subcategory of prey deception. In these instances, the orchid will mimic an insect that is a common prey of the pollinator; when the insect attempts to attack (and devour) what it thinks is a meal, it unwittingly pollinates the flower. One of the more recently discovered (in 2009), and arguably most unusual, examples can be found in the rewardless orchid *Dendrobium sinense*, which is native to the Chinese island Hainan. These flowers are pollinated by the hornet wasp, *Vespa bicolor*. In order to attract the wasps, the flowers will emit a chemical signal that mimics the alarm call of honeybees – which just happen to be the wasp's favourite food. The hungry wasp will charge at the orchid flower, believing it to be a honeybee, and in doing so pollinate the flower.[13]

Some orchids (such as *Epipactis helleborine* and *E. purpurata*) enact a complex 'bait and switch' strategy of food deception. For example, the orchid will attract wasps by signalling that it has insect larvae on offer. Of course, when the hungry wasp arrives, there are no larvae for them to eat. However, these flowers actually do produce nectar, which happens to be the wasp's second favourite food, so they will drink the nectar, and, in doing so, will pollinate the flower.[14]

Enemy deception

Enemy deception (also known as pseudo-antagonism) involves the mimicking of invading insects, which activate the territorial instincts of certain bees. Several orchid species exploit this scheme, through the use of various visual clues, and most significantly by the manner in which they vibrate in the wind. These visual enticements are enough to cause the bees to mistake the flowers for enemy insects and they will attack these 'adversarial flowers', pollinating them in the process. Several species of *Tolumnia* and *Oncidium* (including *Oncidium hyphaematicum*, *O. stipitatum* and *O. planilabre*) use this strategy. In these instances, it is remarkable that despite the aggressive attacking gestures by their pollinators, the orchids are nevertheless able to entice the bees to strike at them at such an exact angle that the pollinia can be attached precisely onto the bee's head.[15] One study has suggested that perhaps the bees do get something out of this activity, in that they become better fighters and defenders of their territory after repeated (but non-lethal) practice runs.[16]

Shelter imitation

Several orchid species engage in shelter imitation; that is, they are pollinated by insects that use the orchid flowers as places to shelter. The insects might use these accommodations as a place to sleep for the night, or simply a temporary hiding place during windy or rainy weather. It has also been suggested that the insect might use these floral refuges for thermoregulation, as the temperature inside the flower can be, on average, several degrees warmer than the outside ambient temperatures.[17] Although this might not qualify as outright deception (and the insect does certainly benefit from

Paphiopedilum orchid cultivar.

the arrangement), these flowers do lure the insects away from their regular sheltering sites during the limited period that the flowers are in bloom. Male bees can often be found sheltering in the butterfly orchid (*Anacamptis papilionacea*), and both male and female bees will shelter within the flowers of *Serapias cordigera*.[18]

Brood-site deception

Brood-site deception describes orchids that attract female insects looking for an ideal site to lay their eggs. Through the use of mildly fetid smells and visual cues, the orchid flowers will mimic such substances as carrion or fungi. These sites would be, if they were real, perfect for laying eggs as they would provide an ideal food source for the developing larvae.[19] *Dracula* orchids, which to us humans can look like little monkey faces, appear to their insect pollinators as little mushrooms. The insects will lay their eggs at the base of the flowers' 'mushroom-like' labellum. Another orchid species, *Brassia arcuigera*, looks like a spider to its female wasp pollinators. Thus, the wasp will attempt to paralyse the 'flower spider' with its sting, and then lay its eggs upon the flower, hoping that when their eggs hatch, the developing larvae will be able to feast on a comatose 'spider'.[20]

Sexual deception

By far the most extraordinary strategy of deception, and one that is only found in the orchid family, is sexual deception. Orchid sexual deceit usually involves an orchid flower mimicking the appearance of a female insect, and doing so in such a convincing manner that the male insect will attempt to mate with the flower. This process of attempted mating has come to be known as pseudocopulation; and as the insect tries to do so, it will unwittingly pollinate the flower.

Sexual deceit tends to be much more targeted than food deception (which might attract a wide range of insects). A well-targeted sexual deception will only attract the males of one particular insect species.

Interestingly, some orchids, such as *Ophrys lupercalis*, may attract several different species of male bee, but there is what amounts to a physical 'compatibility filter' within the orchid's design. Because of this, only a correctly sized insect (in this case, *Andrena nigroaenea*) will be able to collect the pollinia while it attempts to copulate with the flower. This ensures that there is a regulated species specificity in the pollination process.[21]

There are numerous ways that a flower can go about deceiving an insect. The overall shape of its flower, its scent, its coloration and pattern (including those colours outside of our human vision), the way it moves in the wind, and its tactile nature (how it feels to the insect) can all play a combined role in sexual deception. Even the smallest of details may play a significant part. For example, scientists have recently been able to observe, with the aid of a scanning electron microscope, very subtle 'micro-adaptations' that the orchids employ to help fool their male pollinators. These very slight micro-textures are thought to add significantly to the believability of these 'false females' and effectively 'reinforce the behaviour of the "rutting" male insects'.[22] An orchid flower's strategy may also include the releasing of pheromones, which serve as long-range attractors. In many cases, the male insects will find these flower pheromones more attractive than those produced by the female insects.[23]

To our human perception, an orchid flower may not seem much like a female insect. However, we are not able to fully appreciate the aggregate complexity of the orchid flower's deception. Clearly the insects are fooled, and in fact the orchids do such a convincing job of emulating a female insect that the insect's act of pseudocopulation may last up to thirty minutes or more and often culminates with the insect ejaculating onto the flower.[24] According to studies, there seems to be a correlation between lengthier pseudocopulation activity and greater reproductive success (for the orchids, of course, not for the insects).[25]

One of the more remarkable instances of sexual deception involves hammer orchids (*Drakaea* sp.), which are native to Western

Australia. The hammer orchids' labellum looks, to a male wasp, very much like a female wasp. Significantly, the flower's labellum contains a hinged portion that, when extended, works much like a spring-loaded snapping mechanism. When triggered, the labellum arm swings back towards the centre of the flower, flinging the insect onto its column. (One way to visualize this is to stretch your arm out in front of you, with the palm facing upward – imagining that your arm is the flower's

Brassavola cucullata, from *Lindenia* (1887), vol. III.

elongated labellum; when it is triggered, your arm will bend at the elbow and your palm will smack your forehead.) After being triggered, the labellum arm will then slowly extend out again, resetting the trigger mechanism.

Each species of hammer orchid is exclusively pollinated by just one species of male thynnid wasp. Normally, the male and female thynnid wasps have an unusual mating ritual, which coincides more or less with the flowering season of the hammer orchid. During this season, the wingless female wasp will crawl out of its underground home and climb up to the top of a nearby plant where it can openly display itself and emit alluring pheromones. Normally, what is supposed to occur is that the male wasp will immediately be drawn to her. Since she is wingless, and in order to effectively woo her, he will pick her up and fly her to a number of different (non-orchid) flowers that are rich in sweet nectar. After she has feasted on this nectar, he will then mate with her. However, when the hammer orchids are in bloom, chances are that the male wasp will ignore all the available female wasps, and instead be attracted to the deceptive flowers of the hammer orchid. The male wasp will land on the flower's labellum, mistaking it for a wingless female wasp, grab it from the back and attempt to fly off with it. In doing so, the poised flexible hinge of the orchid labellum will fling him back onto the flower's column, where the pollinia will become attached to his back. Shaken, but now laden with the flower's pollinia, he will fly off in search of another 'female wasp'. Chances are he will select another hammer orchid flower and attempt again to carry it off for a prenuptial nectar feast. In a repeat performance, he will be flung back onto this new flower's column and, in doing so, deposit the pollinia that he is carrying onto the flower's stigma. Cleverly, the flowers of the hammer orchid will normally come into bloom just a few days before the majority of the local female wasps are due to emerge from their underground homes. The orchid's opportunistic timing means that they have better success in deceiving the male wasps, as there will be very few actual females in the vicinity.

The lazy spider orchid (*Caladenia multiclavia*) has a movable 'tipping' labellum

We might consider the strategies of sexual and brood-site deception as being especially 'aggressive' forms of deception. With these approaches, the orchid is tapping into some of the insect's most fundamental needs. As a result, the insect feels that it must respond to the signals that the orchid is sending out, or else it will forgo a vital opportunity to procreate or to successfully care for its young.[26] What makes these deceitful strategies seem even more aggressive is that not only will the insects' needs go unfulfilled, they will critically be disadvantaged – the insects will have fewer fertilized eggs and fewer larvae that will survive.

One alternative reading of the orchid's sexual deception is that rather than trying to merely mimic female wasps, the orchids are instead speaking directly to the male wasps, and are seeking to entice them with a more appealing chemical and visual signal than that which the female wasps have to offer. In this way, the orchid will communicate just enough targeted information (both visual and chemical) to trigger the creature's inherent memories and desires. Put simply, the orchid is not trying to be anything that it is not – but it does seek to manipulate the thought processes and behaviours of specific insect targets, and it is doing so in order to benefit itself. This may seem like a rather fine point of difference, but this shift in perspective is actually very significant. Not only does it challenge 'biologists to reconsider how deception evolves',[27] it arguably places a substantial degree of agency upon the orchid. Effectively, a new modified evolutionary model has started to emerge, one which counters the traditional view that two species would have continually, but incrementally, changed in response to the other's adaptations. In the case of orchids and insects, it has been suggested that the insects' morphology and behaviour was already fixed, and it was exclusively the orchids which transformed and adapted in order to exploit what was already present in their environment.[28]

Monica Gagliano suggests that orchids exhibit an ability not just to communicate information about what is actually there, but to express numerous and often complex abstract ideas:

Orchids . . . dupe wasps into becoming unsuspecting pollinators by releasing a spectrum of chemicals very similar to what other plants emit when 'crying for help' to summon predatory insects to feast on caterpillars . . . [and] even mimi[c] animal alarm (pheromone) calls such as those of honeybees, which are frequently captured by wasps to feed on their larvae.[29]

Gagliano describes these as expressions of abstract communication, which effectively shatters our previously held belief that abstraction is the exclusive domain of human thought and language.[30] Similarly, Jeremy Campbell, in his book *The Liar's Tale: A History of Falsehood*, equates orchids with the very human concept of lying. He reminds us that 'orchids mimic the look of female insects, and thus invite pollination by males' and therefore he suggests that 'species flourishing now

Greenhood orchid (*Pterostylis curta*), a terrestrial orchid from Australia.

might be extinct if they had depended on truthfulness to increase and multiply.'[31]

There is some evidence to suggest that orchids may also be involved in deliberate deception with regard to their underground activities. Although most orchids, particularly terrestrial species, forge close associations with mycorrhizal fungi, it is still up for debate as to how much the fungi actually gain from these relationships. In many cases, it does appear as if the orchid gets the better deal (and that this inequitable relationship may be the result of deception). However, there are some instances where it is very clear that the orchid is entirely opportunistic. This seems to occur when a terrestrial orchid entices a fungus that is already in an association with another neighbouring plant species. In connecting with the fungus, the orchid is able to tap into and siphon off carbon and sugars that are flowing between it and the neighbouring plant.[32]

Pitfall Orchids

Some orchids will not only deceive their insect pollinators but trap them within their modified floral forms, which might be described as 'pitfall traps'.

To some degree, these 'pitfall traps' echo the form and behaviour of carnivorous pitcher plants (such as *Nepenthes* spp. or *Sarracenia* spp.), which use their modified leaves to trap insect prey. Although the motivations and outcomes are quite different, the techniques used do bear an intriguing resemblance. Carnivorous pitcher plants develop large pitcher-shaped leaves, which normally fill with a combination of secreted fluid and falling rainwater. Insects are attracted to these pitchers (sometimes by a small amount of leaf-secreted nectar), and when the insect alights on the slippery edges of the pitcher they will invariably fall into the liquid contained within. Unable to get out, the insect will soon drown and disintegrate and the pitcher plant will absorb the ensuing nutrients.[33]

Similarly, the flowers of certain orchids (such as the lady's slipper orchid and the bucket orchid) have a modified labellum which takes the form of a large pouch (and in some cases these will fill with secreted fluid and rainwater). The pollinating insect will land on the slippery edge of this pouch, lose its footing and fall in. Unable to get out the way it came in (due to the slippery walls or downward-pointing hairs), it will be forced to travel (or swim) to another exit. As it squeezes through the narrow passageway to freedom, it will be forced to come into contact with the flower's column and therefore either receive or transfer pollina.

The large spotted flowers of *Stanhopea tigrina* attract male euglossine bees, which will visit the flowers in order to collect fragrances. As they collect the waxy fragrance-rich compounds on the edge of the labellum, they will invariably fall into the flower, coming into contact with the pollinia. Upon a subsequent visit to another *S. tigrina* flower, they will fall again and deposit the pollinia onto the flower's stigma.

Other instances of pitfall orchids are found among the various species of slipper orchids. For example, the long-tailed slipper orchid (*Phragmipedium caudatum*) attracts its pollinators with the use of a rather foul-smelling fragrance. This odour is emitted from its elongated ribbon-like petals, which dangle down to the ground, wafting their smells into the breeze. Attracted by this odour, a female fly

Phragmipedium hybrid.

Cypripedium wallisii
(syn. *Phragmipedium warszewiczianum*),
featuring long ribbon-like petals, from
Lindenia (1887).
vol. III.

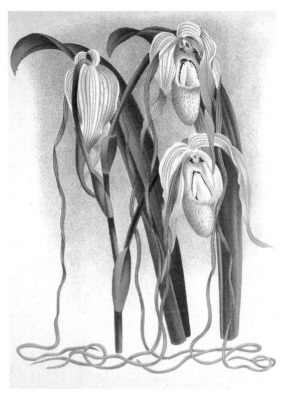

will approach the flower, where it will notice the numerous spots that surround the rim of the flower's pouch. To the fly, these resemble aphids, an ideal food source for their newly hatched larvae. As the fly attempts to lay its eggs, it will lose its footing on the flower's slippery rim and fall into the pouch.[34]

Perhaps the most extraordinary example of a 'pitfall orchid' is the bucket orchid (*Coryanthes speciosa*) of central Panama. The flower secretes its own fluid into its voluminous labellum, which is, as its name suggests, bucket-shaped. It may also become 'topped up' with rainwater; however, as there are overflow holes part way up the sides of the bucket, any excess fluid will drain out. The flower attracts scent-collecting male bees which, while collecting the fragrant oils, will fall into the fluid-filled bucket. After being dunked in the fluid, the insect's wings become drenched and it is unable to fly. Its only escape

CORYANTHES SPECIOSA. VAR.

Bucket orchid (*Coryanthes speciosa*), from James Bateman,
The Orchidaceae of Mexico and Guatemala (1837–43).

route is through the overflow tubes, which lead the insect towards
the column where the flower's pollinia are pressed and glued onto
its thorax. The glue, however, takes about thirty minutes to fully
harden, which coincidentally is how long it takes for the insect's saturated wings to dry out. Once these are dry (and the pollinia firmly
attached), the insect is able to fly away.

As yet, there is no species of orchid that has been proven to be carnivorous. However, there is one species, *Aracamunia liesneri*, found growing in nutrient-poor soil in Venezuela, that is strongly suspected to be carnivorous. Importantly, as with all carnivorous plants, it is the leaves that trap and consume insects – never the flowers. This species of orchid has numerous minute, sticky hairs (similar to those of the sundew plant, *Drosera* sp.) which cover the leaves of the plant, and are where tiny insects become trapped and soon die. It is yet to be determined, however, whether or not the orchid subsequently dissolves and then absorbs the nutrients of these dead insects into its leaves. If this can be proven, then there may well be at least one species of carnivorous orchid.[35]

Mobile Orchids

We often think of plants as being immobile, with the exception perhaps of Venus flytraps or sensitive plants. However, numerous examples of fast movement can be found within orchid flowers. Such mobility may involve a simple hinged labellum that will tip back and forth when an insect lands on it, or it might consist of very sophisticated 'spring-loaded' floral parts that will either aggressively propel the insect into the column, or forcefully slam pollinia against the insect.

One of the most common mechanisms is the hinged or 'tipping balance' labellum. This labellum is activated when an insect alights on it; as the insect walks towards the inside of the flower, it will inevitably pass a balance point, causing it to suddenly tip forward, and the insect will be thrust against the inner column. There are numerous orchid species that feature this mechanism, including *Porpax elwesii*, *Peristeria elata* (the holy ghost or dove orchid), *Specklinia dunstervillei*, *Bulbophyllum lobbii*, *Caladenia multiclavia* and *Grobya fascifera*.

More complex are those orchids that have a 'hair-trigger' labellum. Rather than simply relying upon the shifting weight of the insect to tip the balance and slide the insect into the column, these will release

The dove orchid, or holy ghost orchid (the national flower of Panama), has a hinged lip which will fling a visiting insect into the flower's column, where it will either pick up or deposit pollinia.

A male flower of *Catasetum expansum*. A 'trigger hair' is visible just above the orange protrusion of the labellum; when this is triggered, the flower's pollinia will be actively thrust onto the visiting insect.

their built-up tension to actively fling the insect against the column. After doing so, the mechanism will slowly recalibrate, moving back into place, to be ready for the next visiting insect. Orchids with this mechanism include *Plocoglottis plicata*. However, it is the various species of Greenhoods (such as *Pterostylis curta* and *Pterostylis sanguinea*), commonly found in Australia, that take this to a more remarkable level. These orchid species, in addition to having a hair-trigger labellum, will also capture the insect and trap it within their 'hood' for a period of several hours.

Some orchids, such as *Catasetum expansum*, have very distinctly designed male flowers and female flowers. Both flower genders will offer waxy substances which contain fragrances that the male euglossine bees wish to collect. When a male bee lands on the labellum of the male flower, it will invariably brush against one of its two trigger hairs, which will cause the pollinia to be violently slammed onto the bee. The startled bee will fly away – and it will now avoid the male flowers at all cost. It will instead seek out the female flowers (which offer similar fragrances). Upon visiting the female flower, it will unwittingly deposit the pollinia while it scavenges for the flower's scent substances.[36]

Living Underground

There is perhaps nothing as evocative of a secret life and a clandestine lifestyle than to be 'living underground'. In actuality, all terrestrial orchids spend at least a portion of their lives as subterranean plants. It can take, in some cases, several years for an orchid seed to germinate; then to journey through its protocorm stage; and finally, to emerge above the soil as an advanced seedling with photosynthetic leaves.[37]

There are a number of terrestrial orchids that choose to live out virtually their entire lives underground, including those belonging to the genus *Gastrodia* (commonly referred to as potato orchids), which range widely across Asia, Australasia, India and Africa. Most of these

 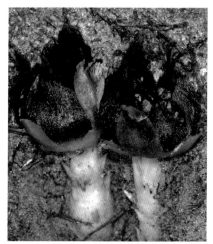

The flowers of two different species of Australian underground orchids: (left) *Rhizanthella johnstonii*; (right) *Rhizanthella gardneri*. Normally growing and blooming entirely underground, these flowers have been partly uncovered in order to be photographed.

(there are nearly a hundred different species) will only be visible when they flower. Their inflorescences can sometimes rise more than a metre above the ground's surface. These plants do not photosynthesize and therefore are wholly dependent on mycorrhizal fungi.

However, there is another extraordinary genus of underground orchids (*Rhizanthella*), which are endemic to Australia. These orchids will remain beneath the surface for their entire lives – and will even flower underground! The first species to be discovered in this genus was *Rhizanthella gardneri*, known as the western underground orchid (and first described in 1928). Because it spends its entire life underground, it is wholly dependent on mycorrhizal fungi. Intriguingly, as this species is only found growing less than a metre from the shrub bush *Melaleuca uncinata*, it is believed that the orchid routinely forms complex three-way associations. In this way, nutrients and carbohydrates are exchanged between the orchid, the bush and the fungus.[38] When the orchid blooms, the small flowers (4–5 millimetres/under ¼ in. in diameter) will sometimes just peek out of the soil, but they will normally remain covered by leaf litter. There is, however, enough of a passageway for its two primary specialist pollinators (fungus gnats and termites) to access the flowers. Once pollinated, the plant will produce very small berry-like fruit – unlike most orchids, these will not quickly dry out, and its seeds are not released to the wind. These bright red berries contain up to 150 seeds each, and are consumed by small rodent-sized marsupials, which after digesting the berries will disperse the seeds through their droppings. There are currently five recognized species of Australian underground orchids in the genus *Rhizanthella* – the most recent, *R. speciosa*, was discovered in 2016. The flowers of this species are also the largest, measuring 15–30 millimetres (½–1¼ in.) in diameter, and are described as having 'a similar appearance to that of a sea anemone'.[39]

Ant-Orchids

Ant-plants (or myrmecophytes) are plants that develop intricate associations with ant colonies. There are a number of epiphytic orchids that are considered to be 'ant-orchids'; particularly those found in the genus *Myrmecophila* (a name that is derived from the Greek words *myrmeco*, which means 'ant', and *phila*, meaning 'love').

Ant-orchids will occasionally employ their ants to serve as pollinators. Pollination by ants is actually quite rare in the plant world, as ants usually produce strong antibiotic secretions (myrmicacin) from their metapleural glands, and this can badly damage the pollen.[40] However, orchids tend to be well suited to using ants as their pollinators because, rather than being composed of powdery grains, their pollen is protected in sticky globs and furthermore these globs are often elevated upon a thin stalk (or stipe), which keeps it away from the ant's secretions.

Most ant-orchids (for example, *Myrmecophila tibicinis*) are used by ants as nesting sites. Because the pseudobulbs of these orchids are mostly hollow, with already intricate chambers and slot-like openings at their bases, they make ideal colony sites. The ants will enter the pseudobulbs through the openings at their base, and use these stems as living quarters and places to raise their young. However, at

SCHOMBURGKIA TIBICINIS.

Schomburgkia tibicinis (syn. *Myrmecophila tibicinis*), from James Bateman,
The Orchidaceae of Mexico and Guatemala (1837–43). This orchid is sometimes
referred to as an ant-orchid, as ants will take up residence in its pseudobulbs.

least one pseudobulb per plant will be set aside for use as the ant colony's waste disposal site. The ants will fill these 'garbage bins' with 'debris that include dead ants, faeces, a variety of insects, pieces of plant material, seeds, and sand'.[41] This in turn breaks down (as there are helpful fungi and bacteria present) and the resulting 'digested' nutrients are then absorbed and utilized by the orchid plant. In this way, the ants essentially feed the orchids. Furthermore, the ants will act as security guards, diligently protecting the plants from attacking herbivore insects.[42] These ants have also been known to protect the orchids from attacking humans. Writing in 1878, naturalist Henry Ogg Forbes described his encounter with these ants:

In tearing down a galaxy of epiphytic orchids . . . I was totally overrun, during the short momentary contact of my hand with the bunch, with myriads of a minute species of ant, whose every bite was a sting of fire. Beating a precipitous retreat from the spot, I stripped with the haste of desperation, but, like pepper-dust over me, they were writhing and twisting their envenomed jaws in my skin, each little abdomen spitefully quivering with every thrust it made.[43]

Another species of ant-orchid is known as the Virgin Mary orchid (*Caularthron bicornutum*) and also provides nesting space within its pseudobulbs for various ant colonies. As with other ant-orchids, the residents provide very effective protection from invading herbivore insects and mammals.

Galeandra baueri, from James Bateman,
The Orchidaceae of Mexico and Guatemala (1837–43).

three

Discovering Orchids
🙢

H umans first 'discovered' orchids many thousands of years ago, long before we thought of them as 'orchids'. Indigenous peoples across the world have continuously engaged with these plants, utilizing them for food and medicine and simply celebrating their unique beauty. For example, the Indigenous peoples of Australia, who have continuously inhabited the continent for some 60,000 years, have traditionally eaten the tubers of perhaps as many as two hundred different species of terrestrial orchids. In South America, the cultivation of the vanilla orchid, which is used as both flavouring and perfume, also stretches back more than a thousand years. And in Asia human involvement with orchids had commenced by at least the Han dynasty (206 BCE–220 CE), when the Chinese nobility began cultivating orchid plants. It was also around this time that the earliest-known Chinese herbal text, *Shen Nong Bencao Jing*, was written, which promoted several different species of orchids for medicinal purposes.[1]

In Europe, the consumption of native terrestrial orchids also extends back thousands of years. However, because many of these native terrestrial orchids exhibited underground tubers that were considered testicle-like in appearance, they came to be referred to by the name *orkhis* ('testicle' in Greek). Significantly, based upon the orchid tuber's appearance, the Greek philosopher and writer Theophrastus (371–287 BCE) detailed the supposed aphrodisiac properties of orchids in his text *Historia plantarum*. Thus, for centuries throughout

Europe and into West Asia, orchids had the false reputation of being aphrodisiacs.

Despite our historic and widespread engagement with orchids, people's awareness of these plants remained provincial. Each culture would be familiar with their own local species, but they would know nothing of the radically diverse orchid species that flourished in distant parts of the world. This, however, dramatically changed when Europeans began to explore and colonize the globe. Hundreds of new and astounding orchid species were discovered in the tropics and transported back to England and Europe (and later America); and subsequently the era of 'orchidmania' began.

Orchidmania

When Europeans first discovered tropical epiphytic orchids, their perception of what an orchid was and what it could be greatly shifted. The flowers of these new epiphytic plants were, on the whole, far more striking and beautiful than their own local terrestrial varieties.

The quest for exotic orchids began to gain momentum when, in 1731, the London-based horticulturalist Peter Collinson received a new orchid, *Bletia verecunda* (syn. *Helleborine americana*), from Providence Island in the Bahamas. The plant bloomed the following year, in 1732. According to Lewis Castle, what made this orchid especially impressive to Collinson was that it was 'a dried specimen' which was not intended to be cultivated, but remarkably, 'the tubers being planted, grew and flowered'.[2] Gradually, additional orchid species were successfully cultivated in England, and by 1789 there were fifteen species of exotic orchids in cultivation at Kew (including *Epidendrum fragrans*, *Epidendrum cochleatum* and *Phaius grandifolius*). Over the next few decades, these numbers increased annually and by the 1830s hundreds of species of 'exotic' orchids could be found growing in England.[3]

There is no exact date in which Orchidmania officially began or ended, but it more or less coincided with the reign of Queen Victoria (1837–1901). Some have also pointed to the year 1818 as

LIMAX AND LIMODORUM.

Fig 1 to 4. The Spinning Slug,
5. Tall Limodorum; from Martyn's Hist. Plant.rar.

The quest for exotic orchids began to gain momentum when, in 1731,
the London-based horticulturist Peter Collinson received a dried specimen
of the orchid *Bletia verecunda* (syn. *Helleborine americana*), from Providence Island
in the Bahamas. Much to his surprise, the plant bloomed. Curiously,
this *c.* 1813 print also depicts several 'spinning slugs'.

being significant, as this was when the British plant collector William
John Swainson sent a large shipment of rare and valuable (non-orchid)
plants from Brazil to the British horticulturalist William Cattley in
London. According to the popular narrative, Swainson had packed
these rare plants with bunches of dried and discarded orchids, as padding material. When the shipment arrived in London, these 'padding

Cattleya labiata, from *Lindenia* (1887), vol. III. This orchid was first bloomed in London by British horticulturalist William Cattley in 1818. The orchid (and the entire genus) was later named after him.

material' orchids flowered, and William Cattley was stunned by their floral display of vibrant pinks and purples. Several years later, in 1824, John Lindley created a whole new genus and named the orchid species *Cattleya labiata* after William Cattley.

Orchidmania, to some degree, echoed the tulip craze (or tulip-mania) that had swept Holland some two hundred years earlier. At that time, tulips had become extremely popular and, as new varieties and colorations emerged, increasingly high prices would be paid. Soon an economic futures market developed in which buyers would speculate on the forthcoming tulip season and agree to pay increasingly exorbitant prices for bulbs, in the hopes that a particularly rare variegated flower might emerge among them. As the market rose, many speculators became enormously wealthy; however, in 1637 the market abruptly and irrevocably crashed and huge fortunes were lost.

During orchidmania, prices also rose significantly; however, the mania for orchids was not nearly so fleeting. One author, writing in 1890, attempted to explain why he believed orchidmania was very different to tulipmania:

> The enormous sums that are often paid for orchids are decried as foolish, and the extravagance is sometimes compared with the craze that once raged about tulips. The two fashions are not to be compared; for there is something real and solid about orchids, which will always give them rank among the finest and most highly esteemed flowers.[4]

There does seem to be something inherently singular about orchids; and a number of reasons have been articulated as to why they became so popular. For one, they generally fit our expectations of what is a 'collectible'; they tend to be small and compact plants which do not take up much space. They are also unique: each plant is one of a kind, and each new species is invariably distinct from another. Of the rarer species, perhaps only a handful would be available at any one time, giving them a distinct air of exclusivity. Most growers were also aware of the great dangers that orchid hunters encountered in order to bring the plants to England; this not only increased the perceived value of the plants but imbued them with an aura of adventure, danger and mystery.[5]

By the mid- to late nineteenth century the price of some orchids had become exorbitant: a single plant could cost the equivalent of an

Odontoglossum alexandre, from Robert Warner and
Benjamin Samuel Williams, *The Orchid Album* (1884).

average annual salary. Orchid auctions were held weekly throughout
London, with collectors bidding fiercely, and willing to pay increasingly absurd prices. In Paris, orchid auctions were also frequently
held; in some instances, rare varieties of *Cattleya* could fetch as much
as 'ten thousand or twelve thousand francs' per plant.[6] However, less
expensive orchids were also available and as a result orchidmania
began to spread through the middle classes.

The Plant Hunters

To meet the growing demand for orchids, wealthy nursery owners
began to send out battalions of plant hunters who would travel to
distant parts of the world in search of vast quantities of orchids.
Competition was fierce, and these orchid collectors resorted to all
sorts of dirty tricks, from outright theft of each other's shipments to
elaborate sabotage. Some collectors would alter maps so as to mislead
about where particularly valuable stands of orchids could be found;

others would purposefully destroy entire orchid populations (when they were unable to carry them all back to the ships) just so subsequent collectors would not find any. There were also tales of rival hunters urinating on orchid shipments as they sat on the docks, waiting to be loaded onto ships, so that the plants would be rotten by the time they arrived at their destination.[7]

The nurseryman Frederick Sander was known as one of the most ardent orchid dealers of the era. He employed, at any one time, as

Odontoglossum harryanum, from *Lindenia* (1887), vol. III.

many as twenty orchid hunters – encouraging them to be increasingly cut-throat in their quests.[8] One of Sander's collectors was a Mr Arnold, who was sent to Venezuela to bring back a large quantity of *Masdevallia tovarensis*, which were fetching extremely high prices in England. On the long journey to Central America, he met a friendly fellow passenger and struck up a conversation. Arnold, not suspecting foul play, told the passenger of his orchid-collecting plans and even where the best orchids could be found. The 'friendly passenger' turned out to be a rival orchid collector who managed to reach the jungles ahead of Arnold and quickly amassed over 40,000 plants of *Masdevallia tovarensis*. When Arnold arrived at the location, he found that virtually all of the plants had been harvested. However, he was able to track down the rival and, while holding him at gunpoint, seized all 40,000 plants and transported them back to England.[9]

Epidendrum macrochilum, from James Bateman,
The Orchidaceae of Mexico and Guatemala (1837–43).

One of the most famous of the orchid collectors was Benedikt Roezl, a botanist and adventurer from Prague, who was also employed by Frederick Sander. Roezl was a large, imposing figure, with a full beard, and an iron hook in place of his right hand (which he had lost in an unfortunate machinery accident in Cuba). He was well known for his determination and his ruthless techniques. Over the span of his forty-year career, he is said to have discovered over eight hundred new orchid species, and collected tens of millions of orchid plants.[10] It is claimed that much of Frederick Sander's success was owed to the work of Roezl.

Orchid collectors would often encounter extreme dangers and hardships on their travels. One hunter, named Carl Roebelin (who was also employed by Sander), seems to have had a particularly rough time on one of his expeditions. There were rumours circulating in London that a new variety of red *Phalaenopsis*, similar to the pink *Phalaenopsis schilleriana* that had recently sold for 100 guineas, had been spotted somewhere within the Philippine islands. So, in 1880, Sander sent Carl Roebelin to collect them. While there, Roebelin found himself in the midst of a tribal dispute, endured a violent hurricane and narrowly escaped being buried alive in a huge earthquake. It is claimed that during the earthquake he was knocked unconscious; when he awoke and opened his eyes, he found himself staring 'face to face' at the rare orchid, *Euanthe sanderiana*. Although these were not the orchids that he had travelled to the Philippines to collect, he did take them back to England and they sold for very high prices. The following year, Roebelin returned to the islands, and this time he did find the elusive red *Phalaenopsis* and collected over 20,000 plants of the species. Unfortunately, on his return to England he encountered another hurricane and all 20,000 orchids were lost at sea.

Orchid hunters routinely had to battle relentless swarms of mosquitoes, fire ants, venomous snakes and wild animals. The renowned orchid collector George Ure Skinner, who had a business interest in Guatemala, recounted how he was frequently attacked by swarms of fire ants as he climbed trees to collect orchids.[11] Skinner also lost a huge number of plants in several catastrophic shipwrecks. Despite these challenges, he made 39 journeys across the Atlantic, but during a brief stopover in Panama he became ill with yellow fever and died in 1867.

As exciting as some of these orchid adventure stories may appear, in actuality the entire era of orchidmania was disastrous for both the orchids and their natural habitats. Each year, habitats were decimated, and hundreds of thousands of orchids ripped from their natural habitats and unceremoniously shipped off to England, Europe and North America. Orchid hunter Albert Millican callously wrote,

> In those immense forests, cutting down a few thousands of trees is no serious injury; so I provided my natives with axes and started them out on the work of cutting down all trees containing valuable orchids . . . After about two months' work we had secured about ten thousand plants, cutting down to obtain these some four thousand trees.[12]

Victorian-era orchid hunters with piles of harvested orchids.

To add to the senselessness of this environmental destruction, most of these orchids never made it back alive. Millican added, 'Many of the plants die before they leave the coast, many more before they pass the West Indies; a few reach the Azores, and fewer still arrive in England safely.'[13] Another report describes how Benedikt Roezl once collected 27,000 *Dracula* orchids in Colombia, but only two of these plants made it back to England alive.[14]

Although many have pointed to the early nineteenth-century invention of the Wardian case (which was essentially a portable, suitcase-sized greenhouse) as being a significant development, it actually had very little impact during the frenzied era of orchidmania. While Nathaniel Bagshaw Ward's invention did assist safe transportation of individual specimens (for very wealthy collectors or for scientific study), the majority of orchid shipments did without such first-class accommodations. Virtually all the wild-collected orchids from the era of orchidmania were simply stuffed into bags or crates and shoved into frigid, damp and dark ships' holds, often for months on end.

Discovering (Skull) Orchids

Astonishingly, there has been not one but two instances in which a rare epiphytic orchid has been reportedly discovered growing out of the top of a human skull. Although such a find might be within the realm of possibility, it seems rather improbable that a perfectly healthy epiphytic specimen (which is happiest growing high up in forest trees) would be found growing naturally out of the top of a human skull. It also seems highly unlikely that such a discovery would occur more than once!

The first reported discovery occurred in 1891, when an adventurous plant hunter known as Mr Micholitz travelled to New Guinea to look for the elusive *Dendrobium schroderianum*.[15] While in New Guinea, Micholitz claimed to have found a rare orchid growing in a graveyard and attached to a human skull.[16] Upon his return to England, the skull

It was claimed that this skull was found in the Philippines with
a moth orchid (*Phalaenopsis*) growing out of the top. It was exhibited
at New York's International Flower Show in 1915.

orchid was prominently displayed at Protheroe's auction house in
the lead-up to a major orchid auction. The auction turned out to be a
great success and was described as 'A great day indeed. Very many of
the leading orchid-growers of the world were present, and almost all
had their gardeners or agents there.'[17] No doubt, the publicity gener-
ated by Micholitz's purportedly authentic skull orchid would have
contributed to the sale's success.

Some 25 years later, another orchid skull was reportedly found, under suspiciously similar conditions. This orchid skull was show-cased at the New York flower show in 1915, and not surprisingly it was a feature story in numerous newspapers in the lead-up to the flower show:

> One of the most interesting exhibits at the International Flower show at Grand Central Palace, New York, was a moth orchid growing in a human skull. A rather curious story accompanies the exhibit. The skull is that of an old tribal chief of the Philippine islands, who was murdered forty years ago by Guanu, a Suriago chief, for stealing one of the latter's wives. Guanu kept the skull as a trophy until his death, when it was placed upon Guanu's grave as a tombstone. An orchid took root and as the flower bloomed it was zeal-ously guarded by the natives who thought the orchid was the spirit of their chief. A traveller passing through the vil-lage saw the freak and stole it from the natives and sent it to a florist of Rutherford, N.J. Note how the expansion of the roots has caused the frontal bone to crack. The roots extend down through the skull and can be seen through the nasal cavity and beneath the jaw.[18]

Although it is possible that this news article was a true account of the discovery of yet another rare epiphytic orchid to be growing from the top of a human skull, it is much more probable that it was the work of a wily publicist's skulduggery.

Commercial Orchid Sellers

In the early days of orchidmania, generally only the wealthy could afford to pay the exorbitant prices that orchids would command. Queen Victoria was enamoured of them, and soon virtually everyone in positions of wealth and power had a collection. Fortunately, as one

Orchids growing in a Victorian-era greenhouse.

writer mused, 'The passion for orchids begins as a hobby of the wealthy and powerful; eventually it escapes, a sort of plague of beauty, to infect the hearts of the lower classes.'[19] Certainly, with regard to price and availability, orchids did gradually manage to 'escape' from their predominately elitist position. Conrad Loddiges and, later, his son George are credited with establishing the first major nursery in England that supplied orchids to the general public. In their 1839 catalogue, they offered over 1,500 different species of orchids for sale.[20] Soon afterwards, other nurseries (including the notable Veitch nurseries of London) made available an increasing number of orchid species.

By the late 1860s a number of American nurseries also began selling substantial quantities of orchids. One orchid seller, John Saul of Washington, DC, claimed that 'My prices are very much lower than they can be purchased for in Europe, in many cases not more than one-half, and stronger, and in every respect, superior plants. What are offered there as cheap Orchids are in most cases little pieces.'[21]

His orchid plants were indeed inexpensive for the time; he had for sale over 250 different species, with prices ranging from $1 to $5 per plant. However, local native orchids were being made available at exceptionally low prices. For example, Southwick Nurseries of Massachusetts offered orchids ranging from 20 cents each for *Habenaria blephariglottis* (white-fringed orchid) to the more established 'strong

Anguloa uniflora, from *Lindenia* (1887), vol. III.

clumps' of *Cypripedium spectabile* (which were 'too heavy to mail') for just 50 cents each. Bulk quantities of these native orchids were also available; for example, 1,000 orchids could be purchased for as little as $15.[22]

One of the first successful orchid hybrids occurred in 1853, when John Dominy crossed two species of *Cattleya* (*C. guttata* × *C. loddigesii*).[23] Gradually, others began to have success with hybrids; however, the germination rate remained very low. Nurseryman H. J. Veitch remarked, 'I should say it is far more difficult to raise the seedlings of some hybrid crossings than it is to raise very delicate children.'[24] Towards the end of the 1800s, hybrid orchids were becoming available for sale in limited numbers, but at relatively high prices. For example, the American nursery Lager & Hurrell were offering 'Cattleya × Claridiana' hybrids in 1899 for as much as $50 per plant.[25]

Cut Flowers

By the 1880s, many orchid sellers, particularly in America, began to focus on the sale of cut flowers. 'No fashionable event is "up to date" unless cut Orchids are used in the decorations,' claimed Pitcher and Manda's catalogue from 1892.[26] Initially, the most popular cut flower orchids were *Cattleyas*, but *Cypripediums* (slipper orchids) also became popular. One catalogue advertised: 'No cut flowers blend more charmingly with roses than Cypripediums. They are noble and beautiful in themselves, unique and graceful in form, rich and delicate in coloring, of great substance and durability. Their flowers last for weeks even after being cut.'[27] At this time, the average price for cut orchid flowers ranged from $5 to $15 per box (usually one dozen). However, specific varieties, and at the right time, could attract very high prices. For example, at Christmas in 1877, a New York florist made the news when it sold a single blossom of a holy ghost orchid (*Peristeria elata*) for $10.[28]

There were a few significant events that affected the availability of both cut and living orchids. First, in 1903, Frenchman Noel

Bernard was able to successfully isolate the mycorrhizal fungi of certain orchids. He then placed these along with the orchid seeds into a sterile medium of agar-agar, and nearly all of these orchid seeds successfully germinated. Although this method held great promise, it amounted to a rather complicated and involved process, and one that was out of the reach of many growers. The First World War, of course, greatly disrupted plant-collecting expeditions and the importation of orchids. Added to this, in 1919, the U.S. government introduced strict quarantine laws which prohibited any grower from importing more than four hundred orchid plants per year.[29] Although these events did provide a much-needed reprieve for tropical orchids in habitat, it also provided a strong impetus for the

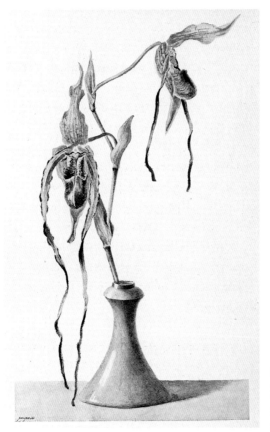

Illustration of cut orchid flowers from W. Watson, *Orchids: Their Culture and Management* (1903).

burgeoning cut orchid industry to develop a more reliable method of seed germination. The answer came in 1922, when the American plant physiologist Lewis Knudson discovered a way to germinate orchid seeds without the need of fungi. He simply introduced nutrients directly into the agar-agar medium, thereby providing the seeds with all of the nutrients (specifically minerals and sugars) that the fungi would normally provide.

By the 1930s, orchids were more popular and more plentiful than ever, and several million cut orchid flowers were being sold each year in the United States. However, by this time there were just a few major producers who had effectively cornered the cut orchid flower market. Thomas Young Nurseries, which held hundreds of thousands of mature orchid plants in its hothouses, is said to have supplied nearly 50 per cent of the commercial market. With very few competitors, the market value of orchids remained artificially high. Average 'retail prices ranged from seventy-five cents (off season, for cheap skates) to $8 and $10 and even $12 (in season) per single blossom'.[30] Writing in 1935, James Agee described the increasing extravagance of the cut orchid mania in the United States:

> A fat lot is added to the purchase price by the fact that satin-covered boxes, many of them in bizarre shapes, and ribbons of velvet and silk and incidental backgrounds of other flowers are used to exaggerate the sacred stature of the orchid as a gift. You can get it in heart shaped boxes for Valentine's Day, for instance; and if you care enough about your dear deceased to want to express your grief in expenditure, you can buy a coffin cover woven of orchids.[31]

Orchid growers were always on the lookout for rare and unusual plants, or ones that appeared to fit with current trends. In 1930, the nursery Lager & Hurrell is claimed to have paid $10,000 for a single orchid plant of pure white flowers.[32] Despite the enormous cost, it was seen as a sound investment as it would reliably lead to many thousands of seedlings; and pure white orchids had become the most sought-after flowers for weddings and other celebrations.

Although there were many flowers that outsold them (such as roses), orchids were regarded as the most elite of flowers. Thomas Young Nurseries promoted the slogan 'Never be without an orchid,' which was soon plastered on the front of every flower shop in New York City.[33] It soon became accepted that 'any florist in the fashionable districts must carry orchids or have people conclude he is not a first-class florist.'[34] By this time, orchid corsages had become synonymous with high society and formal dances. 'One Cattleya with a spray of the Glory fern and ribbon is perfect,' declared a florist's book in 1930.[35]

With increasing tourism to tropical destinations, particularly to the Hawaiian Islands, orchid flowers were soon regarded as an essential Island souvenir. Although very few orchids are actually native to the Hawaiian Islands, their cultivation had recently become widespread as large numbers of Asian workers had migrated to the islands to work on the sugar plantations. When they arrived, they brought with them their prized orchid collections, which flourished in the Islands' climate; and soon Hawai'i became almost synonymous with tropical orchids.[36] As a result, orchids became a primary flower used in making the traditional lei (a wreath of flowers worn around the neck). *Dendrobium* flowers were the most commonly used variety, and frequently these would be dyed, so as to offer the tourist an assorted rainbow of orchid colours.

Although sales of cut orchid flowers continue to be significant today, potted *Phalaenopsis* hybrids have recently become even more popular. Many commercial orchid growers now employ tissue culture techniques to produce literally millions of plants from just a few small tissue samples. This has allowed for the production of vast numbers of nearly identical plants at very low cost. Thus, the once rare *Phalaenopsis* orchid is now available at virtually every plant store and supermarket. In fact, potted *Phalaenopsis* orchids have become so inexpensive and so prevalent that they have begun to impact the cut flower

Poster promoting tourism to Hawai'i. The woman is depicted
wearing an orchid in her hair and holding an orchid-flower lei.

Moth orchid (*Phalaenopsis* hybrid) growing in a pot.

industry. They generally cost the same as (or sometimes less than) a bouquet of cut flowers; but the blossoms of a *Phalaenopsis* hybrid can remain fresh for months – and if cared for, they will soon bloom again. In the United States alone, tens of millions of *Phalaenopsis* orchids are sold each year.[37]

Early Scientific Discoveries

One beneficial outcome of orchidmania was that in the flurry of collecting and hunting for new species of orchids, a number of scientific discoveries were also made, increasing our overall understanding of orchids.

These advances, as well as important information on orchid cultivation, were reflected in a number of publications of the era. One of the first of these was *The Orchidaceae of Mexico and Guatemala*, by James Bateman, which was published between 1837 and 1843. The book is often noted for its impressively large size, its pages measuring 70 × 53 centimetres (27½ × 21 in.). The volume features detailed descriptions of numerous orchid species as well as a wide range of cultural information relating to where these orchids are found throughout Mexico and Guatemala. Aimed towards an elite audience, it also incorporates a good deal of humour, which seems surprising for this type of botanical publication. Most stunningly, it contains forty full-coloured lithographic prints of flowering orchid plants. These were made from the paintings of two established female artists, Miss Sarah Drake and Mrs Withers. The book also includes several pages of horticultural tips and lists a hundred species of 'the best Orchidaceae cultivated in British collections' (as of 1843). Bateman was also a prolific orchid grower and collector and had assisted Charles Darwin by sending him a number of plants for his research on orchids. However, due in part to the failure of his publishing ventures to make a profit, he ended up having to liquidate much of his orchid collection in 1861 to pay off his substantial debts.[38] Another significant publication was *The Orchid-Growers Manual* by Benjamin Samuel Williams, first published in 1852. This was one of the first widely available publications that provided practical guidance on growing both terrestrial and epiphytic orchids. The comprehensive text covered such topics as watering, heating, ventilation, pests, disease, soil, repotting and propagation.

However, by far the most influential book on orchids of the nineteenth century was Charles Darwin's *The Various Contrivances by Which*

Orchids Are Fertilised by Insects, which was first published in 1862, with an expanded second edition coming out in 1877. Darwin's book covers a lot of ground, but as the title suggests, its focus is on orchid pollination. He describes his own methodical studies as well as providing summations of the work of some of his contemporaries. Among other things, Darwin's text focuses on the manner in which orchids move: that is, how the pollinia, once fixed to an insect, will predictably move, over time, in order to enable pollination; and how a number of orchid species possess movable parts within their flowers that also facilitate pollination.

In one section titled 'Power of Movement of the Pollinia', Darwin describes a simple but intriguing experiment that has become known as his 'pencil test'. The experiment involved his careful insertion of a sharpened pencil into a flower, so that its pollinia would become

Aerides fieldingi, from *Lindenia* (1887), vol. III.

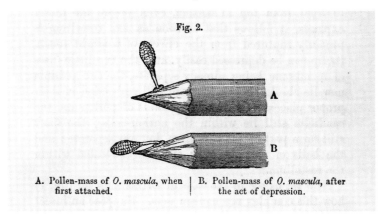

Fig. 2.

A. Pollen-mass of *O. mascula*, when | B. Pollen-mass of *O. mascula*, after
first attached. | the act of depression.

The famous 'pencil test' from Charles Darwin,
The Various Contrivances by Which Orchids Are Fertilised by Insects (1877).
This illustration by George Brettingham Sowerby demonstrates how
orchid pollinia will 'move' from position 'A' to position 'B' after a period of time.

affixed to the pencil tip. He then describes the pollinia changing orientation from a mostly vertical angle to a horizontal one. This 'movement' is caused, not by the pollinia specifically moving, but by the drying-out of the adhesive substance (caudicles). As it dries, it causes the structure to bend forward at a very precise angle, and over an equally precise period of time. Darwin identified that this carefully choreographed movement ensures that the insect does not inadvertently pollinate a flower on the same plant. Since it takes about thirty seconds for this to occur, the insect will have most probably landed upon a flower of another orchid plant, where the desired cross-fertilization could occur.[39] An illustration of this pencil test by George Brettingham Sowerby is included in Darwin's book.

Darwin also describes how *Catasetum* orchids, which he describes as 'the most remarkable of all Orchids',[40] actively propel their pollina onto visiting insects:

> [Nature] has endowed these plants with, what must be called for want of a better term, sensitiveness, and with the remarkable power of forcibly ejecting their pollinia even to a considerable distance. Hence, when certain definite points of

the flower are touched by an insect, the pollinia are shot forth like an arrow, not barbed however, but having a blunt and excessively adhesive point. The insect, disturbed by so sharp a blow, or after having eaten its fill, flies sooner or later away to a female plant, and, whilst standing in the same position as before, the pollen-bearing end of the arrow is inserted into the stigmatic cavity, and a mass of pollen is left on its viscid surface. Thus, and thus alone, can the five species of Catasetum which I have examined be fertilised.[41]

Darwin describes further movements within various other species of orchids, such as in the Australian terrestrial orchid *Pterostylis longifolia*:

The distal portion of the labellum affords a landing-place for insects . . . but when this organ is touched it rapidly springs up, carrying with it the touching insect, which is thus temporarily imprisoned within the otherwise almost completely closed flower . . . The labellum remains shut from half an hour to one hour and a half, and on reopening is again sensitive to a touch . . . An imprisoned insect cannot escape except by crawling through the narrow passage formed by the two projecting shields. In thus escaping it can hardly fail to remove the pollinia.[42]

Darwin's description of these fast-moving orchids provided another stunning example of how plants are not the inert forms that we often consider them to be.

Perhaps most notably, Darwin speculated on what sort of insect was responsible for pollinating the unusual orchid from Madagascar, *Angraecum sesquipedale*. This flower, which had been given to him by James Bateman, features a remarkably long nectary tube, measuring some 30 centimetres (12 in.) in length. Initially, the flower greatly puzzled Darwin, as he pondered what type of creature would be able to drink the nectar held at the base of these long tubes. He eventually concluded that there must be a moth, native to Madagascar, with a proboscis of 30 centimetres or more in length.[43] Initially, many dismissed this theory, but in 1907, a moth with a 30-centimetre proboscis was identified in Madagascar. The moth was named *Xanthopan morganii* subspecies *praedicta* – the 'praedicta' referencing how Darwin had, nearly fifty years earlier, predicted that such a moth would one day be found.

Discovering Deception

Although Darwin was able to detail an exceptional array of 'contrivances' by which orchids are pollinated, he did not support the theory that orchids could engage in any sort of deceptive pollination practices. Darwin was aware that others had conducted investigations in this area – even dating as far back as 1793 when Christian Konrad Sprengel described how some orchid flowers, by not providing nectar rewards, were most likely misleading their pollinators.[44] In fact Darwin stridently dismissed Sprengel's claims, stating:

> Sprengel calls these flowers 'Scheinsaftblumen', or sham-nectar-producers; he believes that these plants exist by an organised system of deception, for he well knew that the visits of insects were indispensable for their fertilisation. But when we reflect on the incalculable number of plants which have lived during a great length of time, all requiring that insects should carry the pollen-masses from flower to flower in each generation; and as we further know from the number of the pollen-masses attached to their proboscides, that the same insects visit a large number of flowers, we can hardly believe in so gigantic an imposture.[45]

Darwin concludes his refutation by adding, 'He who believes in Sprengel's doctrine must rank the sense or instinctive knowledge of many kinds of insects, even bees, very low in the scale.'[46] However, as we now have undisputable and widespread evidence of orchid deception, it might be more useful to consider the ingenuity of the orchid's deceit, rather than any perceived lack of intelligence on the part of the insect. Even the most intelligent of us might succumb (even repeatedly) to a well-crafted ploy. As Danielle Clode has rather humorously pointed out with regard to the pervasiveness of sexual deception in Australian orchids, 'Perhaps Darwin might have had more luck solving some of these mysteries if he'd looked for more orchids when he was in Australia, instead of platypuses.'[47]

'Sham-nectar-producers' is one thing, but the idea of a sexual sham (or pseudocopulation as it came to be called) elevated the idea of orchid deception to a whole other level. As a precursor to the discovery of the orchid's use of sexual deceit, several scientists had observed odd and even aggressive behaviour between insects and various European orchids. Writing in 1829, Gerard E. Smith described how some observers had 'frequently witnessed attacks made upon the bee orchid by a bee, similar to those of the troublesome *Apis muscorum*'. But it was not until 1916 that the French-Algerian Maurice-Alexandre Pouyanne first described (in French) how such 'attacks' were actually the insect attempting to mate with the flower and the result of sexual deception.[48] In 1925, Colonel Masters John Godfery published an article that supported Pouyanne's theories.[49]

However, it was Edith Coleman who significantly advanced the scientific study of sexual deception in orchids. Coleman was an Australian schoolteacher who had an enduring and passionate interest in native plants and animals. It was in 1927 that she observed, at first hand, wasps seemingly attempting to copulate with the orchid flowers. Over the next few years, Coleman would meticulously study the insect's behaviour and went on to publish a number of articles which detailed her findings. Coleman's work effectively demonstrated that male wasps were engaging in sexual activity with orchid flowers. This, she concluded, was in part based on their 'resemblance to a female wasp', noting that 'Even to our eyes, the likeness

Print of *Pleione maculata, c.* 1900.

is apparent. To the inferior eyesight of the insect, the resemblance may be still more convincing.'[50] Another significant aspect of her research was to demonstrate that the orchid flowers also use scent to attract the male wasps.

A few years later, in 1935, it was the Australian entomologist Tarlton Rayment who, in his book *A Cluster of Bees*, first used the term 'pseudocopulation' to describe the behaviours that Coleman had been studying. Prior to this, the term was more frequently used to describe (non-conventional or external) copulation between animals or insects of the same species. As Danielle Clode has pointed out, pseudocopulation in 'relation to orchids and wasps is slightly different. Here the behaviour is intra-specific. An unrelated third party is the one copulating, and yet it is the orchid that is fertilised.'[51] Later, in 1937, Oakes Ames published his paper 'Pollination of Orchids

Zygopetalum cultivar.

through Pseudocopulation', which further cemented the term with regard to the orchid flower's practice of sexual deception.

The idea of pseudocopulation, although well grounded in scientific theory, has also found its way into more philosophical discourse. In their book *A Thousand Plateaus*, French philosophers Gilles Deleuze and Félix Guattari use the relationship between the wasp and the orchid to critique our common understanding of the concept of 'mimicry'. They argue that 'Mimicry is a very bad concept, since it relies on binary logic to describe phenomena of an entirely different nature.' Thus, an orchid does not reproduce a wasp, but rather goes part way in suggesting it – providing merely 'a tracing of a wasp'.[52] More complex still, they use the wasp and the orchid to illustrate their philosophical idea of 'becoming':

The line or block of becoming that unites the wasp and the orchid produces a shared deterritorialization: of the wasp, in that it becomes a liberated piece of the orchid's reproductive system, but also of the orchid, in that it becomes the object of an orgasm in the wasp, also liberated from its own reproduction. A coexistence of two asymmetrical movements that combine to form a block, down a line of flight that sweeps away selective pressures. The line, or the block, does not link the wasp to the orchid, any more than it conjugates or mixes them; it passes between them, carrying them away in a shared proximity in which the discernibility of points disappears.[53]

Deleuze and Guattari are suggesting that the pseudocopulating actions of the wasp and the orchid create a new shared reality in which both the wasp and the orchid essentially transform into something 'other'. They each shed their original identities and edge partially toward the other; the orchid becomes wasp-like and the wasp becomes orchid-like.

Paphiopedilum cultivar.

four
Picturing Orchids

Humans seem to be naturally attracted to flowers; we respond positively to their vibrant colours, sweet fragrances and engaging forms. Several studies have sought to determine which flower varieties humans find more appealing. Most of us, it seems, find flowers with radial symmetry (daisies or roses) to be initially more appealing than flowers with bilateral symmetry (such as orchids). However, once we become familiar with bilaterally symmetrical flowers, they can evoke a greater level of interest and thus a stronger and longer-lasting attraction.[1] To some degree, this parallels how insect pollinators respond to flowers. Flowers with radial symmetry tend to attract a much wider range of insects; bilateral symmetrical flowers tend to attract a much narrower range of insects, often, however, resulting in a more loyal relationship.

It is interesting to consider that even though the attraction 'signals' that flowers send out are intended primarily for their pollinators, humans also find them appealing. Of course, orchids do not really care what we think of them or how we identify with them – they are speaking to their specific pollinators, and not speaking to *us*. When we look at an orchid, we are, in effect, merely eavesdropping (and most probably completely misreading its intended communication). Therefore, it is up to us to try to interpret the nebulousness of the orchid's discourse – and each of us will probably do so slightly differently.

A significant reason why we are attracted to orchids is that we often *see* things within their floral forms. This is due to their unusual use of bilateral symmetry, something that is much more common in the animal kingdom (our faces, for example, exhibit a very clear bilateral symmetry). Bilateral symmetry inherently contains a great deal of complex, but carefully structured, visual information. When we encounter something with bilateral symmetry, we are more apt to recognize it not only as something discrete but as something alive.

We might consider the famous Rorschach test as a parallel to how we read meaning into the bilateral symmetry of the orchid flower. Named after the Swiss psychologist Hermann Rorschach, this is a visual psychological test, involving large ink blots (made from either black or coloured ink). The viewer is asked to look at one of these ink blots and to describe what they 'see' in the abstract configuration, thereby providing an insight into the viewer's emotional or cognitive states. Importantly, these ink blots are images that have been carefully created by applying a 'blot' of ink to the centre of a page, and then folding the paper vertically and pressing the halves together. The result is a unique but also a perfectly bilaterally symmetrical form. Although these ink blots can be widely interpreted, because of their symmetry most viewers will recognize them as *something*; perhaps a creature or a human (or even an orchid flower). Contrastingly, if the ink blots had been made into a form of perfect radial symmetry, we would probably struggle to see anything beyond a mere geometrical shape; and if they were purely amorphous, without any kind of symmetry, we might also struggle to perceive anything beyond a splash of ink.

George Hansen, writing in his 1895 publication *The Orchid Hybrids*, decries the predictable radial symmetry of most flowers: 'What is a [lily flower] but an ornament? which, fine and beautiful as it may be, is and remains nothing but an embellishment, a rosette. Turn it whichever way you please, it appears the same from any side, and does not enable you to tell which is top or bottom.'[2] Next he enthusiastically describes the unique morphology of the orchid:

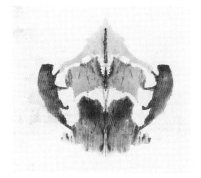 

Original Rorschach test, ink blots (numbers 8 and 9)
from 1921. These ink blots can be interpreted in many different
ways, but because of their near perfect bilateral symmetry most
will recognize them as something: a creature, a human — or,
in the case of these examples, perhaps even an orchid flower.

How different an orchid! Present it in any position you
choose, it can be told without hesitation: this way she was
attached to the spike, this is the way she looks at you, and
there is no margin for doubt about it. They look at us, indeed
they have faces, and so many thousands and hundred thousands of orchids with which I have been face to face, I never
yet tired to again and again study the character of their kind.[3]

Writing a few years earlier, in 1881, M. C. Cooke noted that orchids
have been termed the 'monkeys of the vegetable world' – but he argues
that this designation is not good enough. Monkeys, he points out, 'may
perform fantastic tricks' but unlike orchids they 'do not assume fantastic forms'.[4] Cooke goes on to proclaim, 'So wide is their range of
figure, and so perfectly bizarre are many of the shapes in which they
appear, that one is tempted sometimes to believe they are animated
creatures under some strange disguise of enchantment.'

Orchids do seem to resemble (at least to our contemporary
human eyes) a whole range of creatures. There is even an orchid that
assumes the form of a monkey, *Dracula simia* or the monkey-face
orchid. Appropriately this orchid's species name is *simia*, which translates as 'monkey' from the Latin. The 'monkey' face is comprised of

Monkey-face orchid (*Dracula simia*), from *Lindenia* (1887), vol. III.

minute petals (which form the eyes) and a swollen labellum (which forms the mouth), and these are encased in large prominent sepals (forming the monkey's head). In this case, the flower attracts fungus gnats, which mistake it for a mushroom where they seek to lay their eggs. There is also an orchid known as the flying duck orchid (*Caleana major*), whose flowers look like a duck in flight; as does the woodcock orchid (*Ophrys scolopax*), which from the side also looks like a miniature duck taking flight. Another bird-shaped orchid is the egret orchid (*Pecteilis radiata*), which looks very much like a heron or egret displaying its graceful white wings.

One orchid that has intrigued many since its discovery is the dove orchid or holy ghost orchid. Its compact white flower has a labellum and column that looks like a white dove, with a bowed head and partly opened wings. Because of its resemblance to a white dove, some have attributed Christian symbolism to the flower. Writing in 1868, C. M. Tracy said that those with 'faith', upon first discovering this flower, 'should have paused, awe-stricken at the first view, and murmured in a half-whisper, "Ecce Spiritus Sanctus!"'[5] However, M. C. Cooke, writing a few years later, took a slightly different view. He warned that some have become too enamoured with this orchid flower and have forgotten what it symbolizes: 'But it is the flower alone I fear they worship . . . the image only is bowed down to, not He who made it.'[6]

Humorous illustration created by 'Lady Grey of Groby'
depicting an array of personified orchid flowers, from
James Bateman, *The Orchidaceae of Mexico and Guatemala* (1837–43).

In the concluding section of James Bateman's *The Orchidaceae of Mexico and Guatemala*, the author muses,

> Accustomed as we are to look upon the animal and vegetable kingdoms as altogether distinct, our astonishment may well be awakened, when we see the various forms of the one appropriated by the flowers of the other; and yet such encroachments are but a part of the liberties which these Orchidaceae are perpetually taking.[7]

Bateman includes a humorous cartoon illustration, created by 'Lady Grey of Groby', depicting a grouping of personified orchid flowers. These include a witch on a broom, derived 'from a flower of *Cypripedium insigne*', and a number of other spirit creatures that are 'composed of *Brassia lauceana*, *Angroecum caudatum*, and *Oncidium papilio*'. The illustration also features orchids appearing as various walking and flying insects, including 'a pair of *Masdevallias* dancing a minuet' and a number of '*Epidendra*' who behave 'not unlike the "walking leaves" of Australia'.[8]

Early European Representations

European representations of orchids stretch back more than 2,000 years. One such example can be found sculpted into the floral frieze of the early Roman *Ara Pacis* (Altar to Peace) built by Augustus in 9 BCE, where two different orchid species have been identified: *Cephalanthera* sp. and *Spiranthes spiralis*. Also on this same architectural structure, there can be found a patterned representation of the labellum of *Ophrys* sp.[9] Numerous other orchid sculptures have been identified within several other Roman ceilings and cornices dating from the first to the fourth century CE.[10] It is believed that these representations of orchids were intended to symbolize fertility and 'new life'. Although there have been many recent discoveries of orchid imagery dating from antiquity, it does seem that their depiction later fell out of fashion in Europe. There has been some speculation that this may have been due to how orchids began to acquire a decidedly 'masculine' identity.[11]

Orchids were prominently mentioned in early Greek herbals such as *Historia plantarum* by the Greek philosopher and writer Theophrastus (371–287 BCE). Given that these texts described the plants as having strong aphrodisiac properties, it is not surprising that stories emerged which perpetuated this theme. One particularly influential story appeared in 1706 in a popular gardening book by French writer Louis Liger. The author described a number of different garden plants, and included a moralizing or mythical tale about each variety. In his description of terrestrial orchids (specifically the *Orchis* genus), he invented an origin story which featured a character simply named Orchis. Liger set the story within the realm of Greek mythology, describing how Orchis (a reputed womanizer) attends a party and while there attempts to rape one of the priestesses. As a consequence, he is immediately attacked and killed by others in attendance. Later, his distraught father prays to the gods to have pity on his son and to bring Orchis back to life. However, 'all that his Father could obtain of the Gods, was to have him turn'd into a flower, which was the perpetuate of his name, as a lasting stain upon his memory.'[12] This, according to Liger's tale, is why terrestrial orchid tubers look like testicles. Surprisingly, this origin story has been repeated so often over the past three hundred years that it is now frequently misconstrued as being an authentic ancient Greek myth, rather than merely an anecdote published in an eighteenth-century French gardening book (and credit is due to author Jim Endersby for reminding us that there is, in fact, no character in Greek mythology with the name of Orchis).[13]

Despite the enduring and misplaced reputation that orchids had become saddled with, early European Christians chose to imbue the plants with their own unique mythology, thereby significantly recalibrating their meaning. Instead of fixating upon their underground tubers, early Christians were inspired by the coloration of their leaves. As a number of terrestrial orchids (*Orchis mascula* being one) feature

Thomas F. Collier, *Purple Orchids and Primroses*,
c. 1855–74, watercolour. Note the spotted leaves of the orchid,
which some have attributed to the blood of Christ.

rust-purple spotted leaves, it was suggested that these spots were the
result of Christ's blood sprinkling down upon the orchids that spon-
taneously grew at the foot of the cross.[14] In England, many began to
refer to these leaf-spotted orchids as 'gethsemane orchids', named
after the garden where Jesus and his disciples gathered.[15]

The gethsemane orchid makes a notable appearance in one of the tapestry panels of what are collectively referred to as the *Unicorn Tapestries* (anonymous, *c.* 1495–*c.* 1505). Although potentially containing multiple storylines, the tapestries have frequently been interpreted as a retelling of the Passion of Christ; but as with many early Christian narratives, this one incorporates remnants of a pagan heritage. There are over a hundred species of plants that have been identified on this series of seven tapestries.[16] One of these is an orchid, *Orchis mascula* (known as early purple orchid or gethsemane orchid), which is prominently featured in the final tapestry, *The Unicorn in Captivity*. In this panel, the unicorn, which had been trapped and killed in the other tapestries, is now resurrected but remains in captivity. Although the scene is replete with plant life, it is the orchid that is situated most prominently at the very centre of the tapestry and is the only plant that significantly overlaps with the figure of the unicorn. Given this, it is clear that the unicorn and the orchid are intended to have a close association. In this tapestry, the resurrected unicorn's wounds are still visibly dripping blood. Thus, the unicorn, as Christ, spills out its blood, presumably staining the leaves of the orchid plant.

Orchids are also referenced in William Shakespeare's *Hamlet* (*c.* 1599). In Act IV, scene 7 of the play, Gertrude, the queen, describes finding the dead body of Ophelia floating in a river and conspicuously covered in garlands of flowers. Orchids are included within this description, and they (and the other flowers) are intended to have significant meaning. Here is the passage which describes the floral garland that was found floating with Ophelia's body:

> There with fantastic garlands did she come,
> Of crow-flowers, nettles, daisies, and long purples,
> That liberal shepherds give a grosser name,
> But our cold maids do dead men's fingers call them.[17]

In Gertrude's description, the phrase 'long purples' refers to the tall spike of purple flowers of several common British terrestrial

orchids belonging to the genus *Orchis*, which she clarifies are known by 'a grosser name' by 'liberal' (implying lowbrow and peasant) shepherds. This 'grosser name' would have been 'dog's stones' in reference to the testicle-like tubers of *Orchis mascula*. However, other species of *Orchis*, such as *Orchis latifolia* (syn. *Dactylorhiza maculata*), have roots that look more like the fingers of a hand; thus Gertrude clarifies that the

(left) *The Unicorn in Captivity*, from the *Unicorn Tapestries* (anonymous, c. 1495– c. 1505), with detail (right) of the *Orchis mascula* (known as the early purple orchid or gethsemane orchid) overlapping the form of the unicorn, implying that the unicorn's blood has spotted the leaves of the orchid.

more innocent or refined maids would contemplate *these* orchids, referring to them as 'dead men's fingers'.

One early writer, J. Ingram, sought to decode the composition and, importantly, the specific ordering and placement of the flowers that composed Ophelia's floral garland. In his 1868 publication, *Flora Symbolica*, he suggests that the very specific ordering of these flowers can be translated into a narratively prophetic sentence. Thus, 'crow-flowers' are code for 'fair maiden'; nettles symbolize 'stung to the quick'; daisies mean 'youthful bloom'; and orchids (with the hand-shaped tubers) can be interpreted as 'the cold hand of death'. Therefore, when these decoded phrases are strung together in their appropriate order, Ophelia's garland articulates a sentence that is emblematic of her tragic fate: 'A fair maid, stung to the quick; her youthful bloom under the cold hand of death.'[18]

Orchids in Traditional Asian Art

In Asia, a different emphasis and set of symbolisms emerged. In this region, the focus tended to be on the attractive fragrance, the wispy grass-like leaves, and the delicate beauty of the orchid's floral petals. In Chinese, the orchid is known as *Lán* (or *Lánhuā*), and *Lán* subsequently became a popular name. Orchid also came to be used as an adjective; thus, 'orchid friend' would refer to a very good and trusted friend.[19]

In China, orchids have been cultivated and celebrated for nearly 2,000 years. Yet it was during the latter part of the Ming dynasty (1368–1644) that orchids became particularly renowned within the concept of 'four noble plants' (plum blossom, orchid, chrysanthemum and bamboo) and became an important part of 'Chinese literati art'.[20] Within this context, the orchid was regarded for its beauty and harmony; but it also symbolized 'integrity, nobility, humility, and self-restraint'.[21] It is primarily terrestrial orchids that have featured in traditional Chinese painting and ink drawings. Their wispy grass-like leaves and delicate blossoms were simplified as elegant brush strokes.

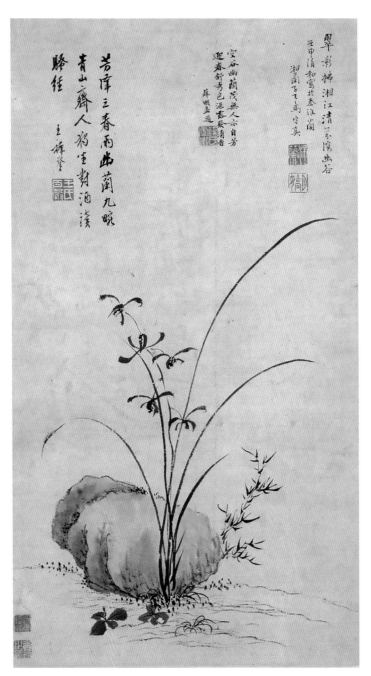

翠影拂湘江清影濕幽谷
壬申清和寫托盖淮山蘭
湘蘭馬守真

空谷幽蘭茂無人亦自芳
迎春舒秀色泡嫩凝清香
薛明益題

若芹三春雨幽蘭九畹
青山齋人獨生對酒讀
騷經
王穉登

Ma Shouzhen, *Orchid and Rock*, 1572, ink on paper (detail).

One significant female artist, Ma Shouzhen (*c.* 1548–1604), was known for her landscapes and particularly her paintings of orchids. In fact, she also went by the name of Xianglan (meaning Orchid of the River Xiang); as with many artists of the era, she was also a poet and a playwright. Orchids figured heavily in her written work as well. On one of her ink paintings, *Orchid and Rock* (1572), the calligraphic inscription reads, 'In an empty valley secluded orchids flourish, unnoticed, but naturally fragrant. Luxurious colors unfurl with the arrival of spring.'[22]

The idea of the four noble plants also made its way to Japan and Korea, where Zen Buddhism further influenced the artists' treatment of orchids.[23] These artists were particularly concerned with creating balanced compositions, which simultaneously underscore a dynamic portrayal of the orchids while maintaining an equally contemplative arrangement. This strong design sense can be found in the work of Satake Shozan (1748–1785). One of his paintings (*c.* 1780) displays an elegant orchid, with wispy green leaves and delicate white flowers; the orchid, tenuously rooted to an outcropping, splays its windblown and slender leaves outward, creating a composition that is at once sprawling and meditative. Later, the Japanese illustrator Tanigami Konan (1879–1928) created dozens of meticulously designed prints

An early Japanese painting of an orchid by Satake Shozan (1748–1785).

Tanigami Konan, *Phalaenopsis Orchid*, *c.* 1917, woodblock print.
Konan's widely published botanical prints were infused with
a striking and carefully designed aesthetic.

of orchids, which were also published widely. Drawing upon trends
of European botanical illustrators, Konan took the standard botanical
image but focused more on vibrant yet balanced compositions, with
pronounced line-work and measured colour choices.

Orchids also had a strong impact on traditional Chinese 'Peking
Opera'. Peking Opera (which first appeared in the eleventh century)
remained relatively unchanged for centuries, but a new performer,
known as Mei Lanfang (1894–1961), emerged in the early part of
the twentieth century. His original name was Mei Lan (*lán* meaning
orchid), but he adopted the stage name Mei Lanfang (this extension
of his surname changed it from simply 'orchid' to refer to 'orchid
chamber' or 'orchid boudoir').[24] He came to specialize in playing female
roles, and is credited with significantly adding to the art form of
Chinese opera. One of the innovations that he brought to the art was
to develop and implement a new repertoire of hand gestures, many
of which were based upon the form and the orientation of orchid
petals. Thus, a type of orchid flower sign language emerged.[25] One
of these gestures, in which the tip of the thumb and middle finger

Detail of a traditional Chinese painting depicting an orchid flower (left), and a corresponding 'orchid flower' hand gesture (right). This orchid-inspired hand gesture was an important element in Chinese 'Peking Opera' and was later adopted as part of everyday Chinese conversational gesturing, as a way to suggest beauty and femininity.

gently touch, became particularly well known in Chinese popular culture, and referred to as 'orchid finger'. In fact, it was so popular that it soon became a normal part of everyday conversational gesturing – and would be used to denote notions of feminine beauty.[26]

Botanical Illustration

As the scientific study of orchids increased, accurate and detailed representations of the plants became essential. A number of detailed engravings of British and European orchids began to emerge in the late 1500s in various books known as 'herbals'. One of the first of these to include substantial orchid imagery was Carolus Clusius's *Atrebatis rariorum*, which was published in Austria in 1583. This was soon followed by another significant and widely distributed text, John Gerard's *Generall Historie of Plantes* (1597). This book describes dozens of different terrestrial orchid species, which the author places under the various groupings of Fox-Stones, Goat-Stones, Dog-Stones and Fool-Stones. The introduction to the section on Fox-Stones not only describes the 'stone'-shaped tubers, but details the manner in which the flowers take on the shape of other creatures:

There be diverse kinds of Fox-Stones, differing very much in shape of their leaves, as also in flowers: some have flowers wherein is to be seen the shape of sundry sorts of living creatures; some the shape and proportion of flies, in other gnats, some humble bees, others like unto honey bees; some like butterflies, and others like wasps that be dead.[27]

The text also includes descriptions of each individual species, accompanied by detailed botanical illustrations.

By the end of the eighteenth and for much of the nineteenth century, botanical illustrations of orchids featured prominently in a number of publications. These printed illustrations expressed vibrant displays, articulating the plants (and particularly their flowers) in exacting detail. *Curtis's Botanical Magazine* (established in 1787) was one

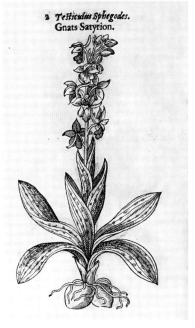

Early Austrian print of an orchid, from Carolus Clusius,
Atrebatis rariorum (1583), depicting its 'hand'-shaped tubers (left); (right)
'Gnats satyrion' with 'stone'-shaped tubers and spotted leaves, as illustrated
in John Gerard, *Generall Historie of Plantes* (1597).

of the more significant publications that made full-colour botanical illustrations accessible to a wide audience; the magazine regularly included illustrations of orchids. Another significant publication was *Paxton's Magazine of Botany*, founded by Joseph Paxton, which also included many colour lithographic prints of orchids. Other notable publications included *The Orchid Album*, published monthly between 1882 and 1892, which included over five hundred colour lithographs; Frederick Sander's *Reichenbachia*, issued annually between 1888 and 1894, which included a total of nearly a hundred large colour lithographs of orchids; and the French publication *Lindenia* (1885–1906), which published nearly a thousand colour lithographs of orchids. One of the most accomplished and prolific illustrators of the unique and varied forms of orchids was Belgian artist Pieter De Pannemaeker. Many of his illustrations were published in the French journal *Flore des Serres et des Jardins*. Horto Van Houtteano also produced a large quantity of highly detailed images of orchids for this same publication.

As botanical illustrations evolved, most artists sought to represent as closely as possible the precise form, colour and size of the orchid plant. However, these were also susceptible to some variance depending upon whether the artist was able to work from an actual living plant or was reliant upon a dried specimen or field sketches made by another artist. The botanical illustrations were also susceptible to a certain degree of artistic licence with regard to how the flowers might be posed, or how the plant might be composed upon the page. Most of these botanical illustrations were intended to suggest that they were growing in their native habitat (implied by perhaps a hint of a moss-covered tree branch); others were depicted as unmistakably domesticated plants, and shown growing from a pot or basket.

German zoologist Ernst Haeckel (1834–1919) created an impressive, albeit creatively designed, grouping of orchid flowers in which he manages to strike an intriguing balance between accurate botanical representation and an elaborately designed grouping of colours, patterns and form. Haeckel, who was very concerned with the interconnectedness and shared origins of nature (and in fact coined the term 'ecology'), clearly promotes this theme in many of his illustrations. In his depiction of orchid flowers from his 1906 publication *Kunstformen der Natur*, he incorporates sixteen different orchid species, which at first glance appear to form a bouquet. However, on closer inspection it is clear that they are intended to be living specimens that simply share a common plant base. Although generally botanically accurate, these dazzling floral forms also seem very animated and full of implied motion, with wavy edges and streaks of colour defining their forms. Because of their front-facing orientation, the flowers seem to imply that they all have faces, which peer out at us. It comes as no surprise that Haeckel, who strongly believed that plants possessed a certain degree of awareness and agency, would imbue his orchids with these touches of personification. Writing in 1901, he asserted that the movements found in various plants such as the Venus flytrap 'are strikingly similar to the movements of the lower animal forms: whoever ascribes consciousness to the latter cannot refuse it to such vegetal forms'.[28]

John Gould (1804–1881) was an English ornithologist who studied hummingbirds and published a number of books with strikingly illustrated plates. One such work, *Monograph of the Trochilidae, or Family of Humming-Birds*, published in five volumes between 1849 and 1861, features hummingbirds interacting with a diverse range of flowers, and includes sixty colour plates that feature orchids. Although he employed a number of artists (including his wife), the majority of the illustrations of hummingbirds and orchids were made by both John Gould and Henry Constantine Richter. Each of these images is carefully designed, many with the shape and posture of the hummingbird echoing the positioning of the leaves and flowers of the orchid. Although both the hummingbirds and the orchids are reproduced in great detail, their context is misleading; most are not actually the flower's primary natural pollinators, as the images seem to imply.

Illustrations and lithographic prints have played a fundamental role in facilitating and disseminating botanical knowledge. However, a two-dimensional print may struggle to truly articulate the morphology

Ernst Haeckel's striking illustration of orchid flowers,
from his *Kunstformen der Natur* (1906).

of a three-dimensional plant. In such instances, a three-dimensional model can be of additional educational benefit. To fill this need, Czech artists Leopold Blaschka and Rudolf Blaschka created a series of three-dimensional plant models made entirely of sculpted glass. This father and son duo produced, over a period of five decades (1886–1936), nearly 4,300 glass model sculptures, including dozens of realistic life-sized orchid flowers.[29] These life-sized flowers, made from blown and flame-worked glass, are extremely accurate in form, pattern and colour. Some of the glass orchids that they produced include *Laelia crispa*, *Odonto-glossum grande* and *Odontoglossum crispum*. These glass orchids are now part of the permanent Blaschka collection on display at Harvard University's Museum of Natural History.

Plate depicting *Thalurania* hummingbirds and the orchid *Oncidium hastilabium*, from John Gould, *Monograph of the Trochilidae, or Family of Humming-Birds* (1849–61). This work features numerous colour plates of hummingbirds interacting with a diverse range of flowers, including sixty that feature orchids.

Orchid Designs

In the late 1800s the orchid had become an important fashion accessory often worn as a corsage and pinned to one's dress or lapel. Due to their prohibitive cost, fresh tropical orchid flowers tended to be the accessories of the wealthy. Yet, even if one could afford an orchid, their availability was severely limited to certain times of the year. Thus, fine jewellery orchids gained popularity as these would serve as perennial alternatives. Initially these brooches were designed in gold or silver; although these successfully maintained an air of exclusivity, they lacked the inherent beauty of the natural orchid flower.

However, this all changed with Tiffany & Co. when in 1889 the company produced a series of orchid brooches which were expertly designed by emerging jewellery maker George Paulding Farnham (who would later become chief jewellery designer for the company).[30] What made these brooches so remarkable was how realistic they were

Tiffany & Co. orchid-
themed brooches, *c.* 1889,
made of gold, enamel and precious
stones (above); and (left) original
sketches by designer Paulding Farnham.

in their design; they were actual size, and exact in their shape and
colorations. The orchid brooches were made of gold, and then enam-
elled in varying colours on both sides and further complemented with
diamonds and other precious gems. Paulding Farnham initially based
his designs on contemporary botanical illustrations, primarily taken
from Samuel Jennings's 1875 book *Orchids and How to Grow Them in India
and Other Tropical Climates*. Then, where possible, he requested actual
examples of these orchid flowers for further study and sketching.[31]
When the orchid brooches premiered in Paris in 1889 they created
a huge sensation. The catalogue boasted that:

> The jeweler's skill in copying nature's forms and colorings
> by the process of modeling and enameling gold, is shown in

the pieces of jewelry imitating several varieties of orchids, which, though almost absolute copies of nature, are not merely artificial flowers, but by peculiar treatment and the introduction of precious stones form unique and artistic articles of jewelry.[32]

Initially, there were 24 different designs made, and in subsequent years similar designs continued to be produced. According to the 1894 price list, Tiffany & Co. brooches of 'Enameled flowers with precious stones' were priced as high as U.S.$150 (equivalent to well over U.S.$5,000 when adjusted for inflation).[33]

By the late 1800s, the proliferation of orchid designs became widespread – appearing on everything from elaborately decorated vases to lamps, furniture and dinnerware. The Minton ceramics factory of Staffordshire, England, produced an extensive range of orchid-decorated plates, cups and vases. Some of these were conventional

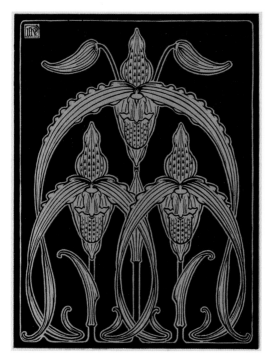

Art-nouveau pattern of *Cypripedium* orchids by Maurice Pillard Verneuil, originally published in Pillard Verneuil, *Etude de la plante: Son application aux industries d'art* (1903).

in design, but a few did stray into the unexpected, such as a brilliant blue bone-china vase from 1872 that depicted a spray of orchid flowers springing from the mouth of a large fish. Orchid flowers also became frequently used in pattern motifs, adorning wallpaper, book endpapers and fabrics. These patterned representations varied from the realistic to the highly simplified and abstract. For example, the French artist Maurice Pillard Verneuil frequently incorporated orchids into his highly stylized art-nouveau designs.

Eventually the orchid began to be represented simply as a colour; which might be regarded as the most sublime and subtlest representation of the orchid flower. The colour 'orchid' is most frequently expressed as a hue which resides somewhere between the spectrum of pink and purple; and it has been used to describe a wide range of products, from clothing to paint. Today, the traditional 'orchid' colour is frequently blended with other hues; thus, paint colours described as 'Orchid Night' or 'Ocean Orchid' have become common. The American crayon brand Crayola has even designated 'orchid' as a crayon colour.

Orchids in Modern Art

Orchids figure prominently in modern and contemporary art practice. As would be expected, their representations are widely varied.

Odilon Redon

The French artist Odilon Redon (1840–1916) created a small painting titled *Orchidée fantastique* (Strange Orchid, *c.* 1910) that features a large white *Phalaenopsis*. At first glance, Redon's orchid looks somewhat like a tree, with a huge orchid flower dominating its branch tops. Near the 'trunk' of this orchid tree, a human figure stands, dwarfed by the immensity of the orchid. On closer inspection, the orchid and surrounding shapes also double to produce a large face. Deep penetrating red eyes are visible on either side of the flower's dorsal sepal, while

Odilon Redon, *Orchidée fantastique, c.* 1910,
gouache and watercolour over pencil on paper.

the flower's labellum forms its nose and mouth. In this reading, the grey tree trunk forms a neck which holds aloft the orchid-head. The human figure appears to be closely associated with the orchid, as is indicated by the scrawled moth form on their chest. It appears that the figure shares a deep attraction with the flower, perhaps even serving as a symbolic pollinator to this 'strange orchid'.

Martin Johnson Heade

The American artist Martin Johnson Heade (1819–1904) was a prolific painter of landscapes, and created nearly sixty paintings that featured large orchid flowers, paired with hummingbirds. The majority of these orchid paintings feature *Cattleya labiata* while a few others showcase *Laelia purpurata* and *Cattleya dowiana*.[34]

Because of their comparable subject-matter, one cannot help but be reminded of John Gould's nature prints, many of which also paired orchids and hummingbirds. Similarly, Heade had also hoped to publish a book on hummingbirds, which would be illustrated with his paintings (although this never came to fruition). However, upon viewing Heade's paintings, it is clear that his landscapes are significantly different in their approach. For one, his paintings feature lush and dense landscapes, and his depictions of orchids and hummingbirds are presented directly in the foreground and in accurate life-size. There is also a noticeable disconnect between the vibrant foregrounded orchids and the more distant backgrounds (which are lush and beautiful). This is accentuated by the fact that the paintings usually contain very little indication of a middle ground, which gives a sense of a portrait that has been incongruously placed against a backdrop.

The orchids appear very much alive, seemingly captured in the midst of an exuberant dance. In fact, the orchid is clearly the most dynamic element – and even though we know that orchids do not visibly move (or dance), they appear very animated. By contrast, the hummingbirds, often depicted in mid-flight (and whose wings

Martin Johnson Heade, *Hummingbird Perched on the Orchid Plant*, 1901, oil on canvas.

represent some of the fastest movements in the animal kingdom), appear far less animated. The orchids sit, at eye level, perched on moss-covered tree limbs, and appear to be looking towards 'the camera'. Perhaps these orchid paintings could best be described as a series of 'orchid selfies'. We could easily imagine these orchids taking their self-portraits (perhaps with the aid of a long selfie-stick), while posing against a variety of lush panoramic backgrounds.

Although Heade had intended these paintings to be ostensibly about hummingbirds, it is unquestionably the orchids that become the focal point. The hummingbirds simply become reoccurring figures that appear to incessantly photobomb each and every one of these orchid selfies.

Marianne North

English artist Marianne North (1830–1890) was a celebrated painter and illustrator of botanical subjects. She frequently travelled the world, depicting the native flora of each locale that she visited. She was also a keen grower of orchids, and, not surprisingly, orchids featured in a number of her paintings. Although some of her orchid paintings were produced on location, many others came from her own substantial collection of tropical plants.[35] Due to her unconventional compositions and bold use of colour, North's orchid paintings rarely appear as posed or domesticated specimens. Instead, they are

Laelia purpurata, the national flower of Brazil. Marianne North, *A Brazilian Orchid*, c. 1880, oil on paper.

more suggestive of snapshots of lush jungle foliage. Her flowers, stems and leaves are freely cropped at the edges of the frame – while other, off-screen, plants are allowed to burst into view. Her many orchid-themed paintings are on prominent display at the Marianne North Gallery at the Royal Botanic Gardens, Kew.

Max Beckmann

Max Beckmann (1884–1950) was a German Expressionist who also included orchids in his compositions. The bulk of his paintings may be divided into two compositional strategies – those that feature heraldic groupings of people, often compressed into restricted quarters, and those that qualify as still-life paintings. However, many of his 'still-lifes' also include a human figure, placed alongside the staged objects.

Particularly in Beckmann's later still-life paintings, he frequently included orchids. Most of these are semi-abstracted renditions of slipper orchids with exaggerated pouches or colourful *Cattleya* flowers rendered in rough strokes of paint. His paintings that feature orchids include *Still-Life on Brown and Yellow (Champagne Bottles and Orchids)* (1934), *Woman with Orchid* (1940), *Orchid – Still-Life with Green Bowl* (1943), *Woman with Mirror and Orchids* (1947), *Still-Life with Orange Pink Orchids* (1948) and *Big Still-Life with Black Sculpture* (1949). At one level, these images can be viewed as simply vibrant and colourful floral-themed still-life paintings; however, since most of Beckmann's paintings seem to be replete with symbolism, it is reasonable to consider that the inclusion of orchids may have intentional enigmatic or erotic overtones.

In a great many of Beckmann's paintings, he has included a mirror in the scene. The mirror is usually situated so that a person or object is visible in its reflection but they are not visible in the rest of the painting space. Thus, we might see a figure portrayed in the mirror's reflection who is not visibly present in the painted scene (perhaps they are standing behind the viewer or 'the camera'); or we might see

Max Beckmann, *Woman with Orchid*, 1940, oil on canvas.

the face of the central figure in the mirror's reflection, but only see the back of their head in the primary painting space. On occasion, however, Beckmann seems to break with the expected optics of a mirror's reflected imagery. For example, in his painting *Woman with Orchid* (1940), the slipper orchid's reflection is actually a repeat of the front view of the orchid that is visible to us (thus we see a duplicate image of its front pouch in the mirror, instead of seeing the back of the flower). Since the optical treatment of the flower's reflection is intentionally incorrect, it helps to further underscore its symbolic nature.

The orchid flower also makes clearly symbolic appearances in some of his other paintings that feature large groupings of figures; for example, a large purple orchid is visible (at the top of a tall pole) in the left-hand panel of the triptych *The Acrobats* (1939), and an abstracted slipper orchid is prominent in *Soldier's Dream* (1942).

Georgia O'Keeffe

The artist Georgia O'Keeffe (1887–1986) is perhaps best known for her large paintings and pastel drawings of greatly magnified flowers; of these, two are of orchids. The first of them, *Narcissa's Last Orchid* (1940), depicts a pure white *Cattleya* orchid, set against ripples and fields of pinks and browns. The title, while humorously referencing the Greek myth of Narcissus and narcissism, was actually devised because the orchid flower used as the model for the painting had been given to O'Keeffe by her friend Narcissa Swift King. The note attached to the gifted orchid read, 'That's the last orchid you'll ever get from me!' Reportedly, Narcissa Swift King had been mildly upset at O'Keeffe, and as a result, O'Keeffe had playfully included her name in the title of the image.[36] The second orchid artwork is simply called *An Orchid* (1941) and was, like the first, produced using pastel on paper, and rendered in wafts of green and white. The orchid depicted in this image is believed to be a hybrid *Cattleya*, perhaps one that has been crossed with *Brassavola digbyana*.[37]

In both of these images, the orchids appear to blend in with the background, making it difficult to discern in some parts where the orchid flower ends and the background begins. It is said that O'Keeffe rejected the exclusively erotic reading of her large floral images (a reading originally insinuated by male art critics), instead wishing to focus on their inherent beauty of form, colour and gradient tone. O'Keeffe prided herself not only on her ability to provide accurate interpretations of the floral form, but on having the patience and understanding to truly appreciate a flower. She once noted,

> Nobody sees a flower – really – it is so small – we haven't time – and to see takes time, like to have a friend takes time . . . So I said to myself – I'll paint what I see – what the flower is to me but I'll paint it big and they will be surprised into taking time to look at it – I will make even busy New Yorkers take time to see what I see of flowers.[38]

As with any abstracted form, the bilateral symmetrical form of the orchid can be open to a wide range of interpretations – but undoubtedly, each of us will see *something* within their floral forms.

Madeline von Foerster

Orchids have featured prominently in the paintings of Madeline von Foerster, a contemporary artist who employs traditional sixteenth-century Flemish techniques of oil and egg tempera to produce meticulously detailed images. Many of her paintings showcase beautiful yet sometimes unsettling images of fauna and flora, including orchids. These often engage with contemporary environmental concerns regarding deforestation, endangered species and loss of habitat. They also seek to address how humans have frequently fetishized certain aspects of the natural world while simultaneously destroying the broader environment. 'We love nature, we kill nature, and we can't quite figure out our relationship with it,' sums up von Foerster.[39]

Madeline von Foerster, *Orchid Cabinet*, 2014, oil and egg tempera on panel.

She describes her artworks as 'living still-lifes, which intentionally use the motifs of that genre to explore our assumptions about owner-ship and objectification of nature. But on a deeper level, they are visual altars for our imperilled natural world.'[40]

One particular painting, *Orchid Cabinet* (2014), alludes to the over-collecting of orchids, and, while showcasing their beauty, also laments their removal from habitat and the implications that this holds for their survival. It displays an interior view of a shipping crate, which encloses a large wooden female figure, carved from black ebony timber. The figure has numerous small compartments, with drawers, carved into it; from these are emitted numerous orchid plants in bloom. Visible in the painting are detailed and accurate representations of eight different species of orchids: *Phalaenopsis hainanensis*, *Houlletia tigrina*, *Vanda coerulea*, *Cattleya labiata*, *Ansellia africana*, *Paphiopedilum fowliei*, *Cypripedium formosanum* and *Angraecum sesquipedale*. Also included is 'Darwin's' moth from Madagascar, *Xanthopan morganii praedicta*, with its incredible 30-centimetre (12 in.) proboscis, which was eventually found to be the pollinator of the orchid *Angraecum sesquipedale*.

The wooden figure represents 'mother nature' but at the same time references the centuries-old museum trend of 'curiosity cabi-nets', which would often house collections from the natural world. These collections, made up of remnants of once living things, often from far-off lands, were intended to educate, and stimulate wonder-ment in, the viewer. An unfortunate aspect of this, of course, was that these once living plants and animals had been removed from their natural habitat to be transformed into lifeless 'objects of curiosity'. In the case of *Orchid Cabinet*, although they appear to be living at the moment, the long-term prospects for these plants are uncertain at best. We are given a clue to this by the inclusion of a note pinned to the wooden figure which depicts a scientific diagram of mycorrhizal fungi. Orchids rely upon these fungi, found in their native habitat, for their germination and growth. The removal of orchids from their natural habitat severs this important life-support system, thereby greatly lessening their chances of survival.

On the interior wall of the shipping crate is visible an airport baggage label, noting the destination 'JFK'. This references the unfortunately too common occurrence of illegal floral smuggling. One of the hands of the figure is detached from the rest of its body, which 'symbolizes our increasingly fragmented and shrinking wilderness, the existential threat to orchids worldwide'.[41] Although the painting's message is stark, the beauty of the orchid flowers is undeniable, which underscores von Foerster's intention: 'I try nevertheless to create beautiful paintings, which provoke reverence and contemplation.'[42]

Debora Moore

Debora Moore is an African American glass artist who is best known for her stunning botanical glass sculptures. Over the decades, the vast majority of her works have been of orchids, which she has been making in glass since the 1980s. She is drawn to 'the astounding variety within the orchid family [which] provides endless opportunities for artistic expression with their vibrancy of color and elegance of form'.[43]

Her orchid flowers are stunning in themselves, but the work becomes especially impressive when we realize that all of the elements of her sculptures, including the supporting 'branches' and 'trees' that the orchids are affixed to, are made completely out of blown and sculpted glass. Unlike the flame-worked glass orchid-models made by the previously mentioned Leopold Blaschka and Rudolf Blaschka, Moore's work is made entirely in the hot-shop, and is furnace-worked, which requires an immense degree of skill and precision in order to achieve the extraordinary degree of detail that her work exhibits.

Moore's emphasis is on uniquely translating 'the breath-taking grandeur and delicate fragility of the natural world into a unique sculptural interpretation'.[44] Her work not only plays with the remarkable forms of the orchid flower, it intuitively plays with the materiality of the glass medium: 'Within each work, glass is used like paint to achieve depth of color. The material's inherent ability to transmit and

Debora Moore, *Blue Lady Slipper — Gigantica*, 2011, glass and silicone adhesive.

reflect light, as well as its variations from transparency to opacity, lends itself perfectly to achieve desired textures and surfaces.'[45] Although Moore's work reflects an accuracy of botanical detail, her focus is less on precise realism and more on capturing an intensely personal experience of natural beauty and wonder.

Marc Quinn

Marc Quinn is a successful and exceptionally prolific contemporary artist who works across a wide range of materials and themes, of which orchids have clearly been a prominent and ongoing one in many of his works. He has produced dozens of huge orchid sculptures; a substantial series of enormous photo-realistic oil paintings that feature orchids; as well as countless smaller sculptural works of orchids. Quinn notes that

> Orchids are like perfectly evolved little sculptures in themselves, they're full of colour, interesting shapes and beauty. Even though they are a plant's reproductive organs, they pun on human ones too. They make you realise it is colour, life and sexuality that keeps the world turning. They are a celebration of life.[46]

Quinn's giant orchid sculptures are particularly striking. Their enormous size and the blatant manner in which they have been decontextualized tend to simultaneously fill us with an astonishing sense of wonder and of unease. Further to this, the incongruous nature of the materials used (namely cast bronze) and the represented delicate nature of an orchid's petals make them 'appear almost weightless and ethereal'.[47]

His equally enormous orchid paintings are stunning in their expression of overly bright vivid colours, replete with pop sensibilities, and meticulous photorealistic rendering. One of these, *Under the Volcano, Slopes of Jan M . . .* (2011; 279 × 419 cm), is rendered in highly saturated colours and depicts a handful of orchid flowers that have seemingly been scattered as a garish garnish atop a mound of bright red strawberries and cherry tomatoes.

five
Pop Culture Orchids
ॐ

Given the immense popularity of orchids, it is not surprising that they have been so widely represented in virtually all forms of popular culture. And, considering their vast botanical and geographic diversity, it is also not surprising that they have been depicted in such varied ways. Orchids have epitomized everything from the exclusive, the beautiful and the sensual to the dangerous and the deadly. They have infused detective and superhero narratives, as well as horror, comedy and romance stories. They have featured prominently too in advertising, politics and all manner of contemporary discourse.

Killer Orchids

Most of us think of orchids merely as beautiful flowering plants. However, some of the earlier popular culture narratives (particularly those emerging in the late 1800s and early 1900s) frequently imbued orchids with decidedly dark and deadly characteristics. This reputation spread quickly and soon became entrenched. One orchid grower, exhibiting at the Chelsea Flower Show in the 1930s, described how

> an elegantly dressed lady, misled by a newspaper article on orchids, enquired the whereabouts of 'the meat-eating orchid'. Without hesitation, the exhibitor apologized for

the absence of this orchid from his stand, explaining: 'it has gone to lunch!' – a reply which appeared to satisfy the gullible enquirer.[1]

It is interesting to note that these popular killer-orchid narratives were inspired by at least two primary sources: one, the exaggerated dangers of orchid-hunting expeditions; the other the exaggerations or misunderstandings of contemporary scientific observation. And

Phalaenopsis, or moth orchid, by Harriet Stewart Miner, from Miner, *Orchids: The Royal Family of Plants* (1885).

of course, each of these sources was augmented with a healthy dose of human imagination.

Undoubtedly, it was Charles Darwin's scientific writings that had some of the greatest impact. In 1862, Darwin published his book *The Various Contrivances by Which Orchids Are Fertilised by Insects* (a substantially revised second edition was published in 1877). This book did not by any means suggest that orchids were carnivorous, but it did imply a certain degree of agency and it did highlight some of their remarkable interactions with insects. Then, in 1875, Darwin published his popular book *Insectivorous Plants*, which categorically demonstrated that there are plants that are capable of luring, trapping and consuming insects (and other small creatures). Five years later, Darwin published *The Power of Movement in Plants* (1880). This book not only demonstrated that plants exhibit far greater movement than most people had been aware of, but it went so far as to suggest that plants possess the botanical equivalence of cognition:

> It is hardly an exaggeration to say that the [plant root-tip] thus endowed, and having the power of directing the movements of the adjoining parts, acts like the brain of one of the lower animals; the brain being seated within the anterior end of the body, receiving impressions from the sense-organs, and directing the several movements.[2]

The idea that plants have significant movement, have agency and particularly that they can be carnivorous truly shook up the public's view of the natural world. Although people had, for example, been aware of plants such as the sundew or the Venus flytrap for centuries and had witnessed countless insects being trapped and dying on their leaves, most had simply assumed that this occurred by accident, or perhaps for defensive reasons.

The shift in public opinion is obvious when we compare what was being written about these plants prior to Darwin's publications to what was said after his books had been published. For example, naturalist Anne Pratt, in her pre-Darwinian book *The Flowering Plants of Great Britain* (1855), sought to speculate as to why so many insects would become trapped in the leaves of the sundew plants (*Drosera*) that widely inhabited nearby meadows. She came to the conclusion that these sundews were simply engaging in the rather noble task of helping to maintain the balance of nature by keeping the insect populations down (of course she refused to believe that they were actually *eating* the insects).[3]

However, soon after Darwin's books were published and it was categorically proven that some plants were indeed eating insects, a very different tone emerged, as is evidenced in J. G. Hunt's essay from 1882. In describing these same sundew plants, he declares:

> I have seen the delicate and painted fly disjointed and crushed, its splendid and wonderful eyes torn asunder by the hungry plants; the little moths, themselves but velvet atoms rejoicing in the warm sunlight, but now slowly melting away, limb by limb, in these horrible vegetable stomachs; their life and marvellous form and startling beauty all wrecked to feed a sundew in one of these Droserian graveyards . . . Surely here, if anywhere, is vegetable wickedness.[4]

Hunt's writing epitomized the growing mistrust of these insect-eating plants. Remarkably, Italian criminologist Cesare Lombroso propelled this mistrust even further when he declared in his 1884 publication *Criminal Man* (third edition) that carnivorous plants were most probably the evolutionary source of human 'evil' and that humanity's propensity for criminal activity stems specifically from these plants.[5]

Significantly, in 1877, scientist and nature writer Alfred Russel Wallace published an article in which he identified how a Javanese mantis insect (now known as the orchid mantis, *Hymenopus coronatus*) uses camouflage to mimic the form and coloration of orchid flowers in order to catch its insect prey:

Orchid mantis (*Hymenopus coronatus*) eating a butterfly.

in Java [there is] a pink-colored Mantis, which, when at rest, exactly resembled a pink orchis flower. The Mantis is a carnivorous insect which lies in wait for its prey, and by its resemblance to a flower the insects it feeds on would be actually attracted toward it. This one is said to feed especially on butterflies, so that it is really a living trap and forms its own bait![6]

The readership of Wallace's article would likely have been limited to the scientific community and excluded the general public. However, two years later, in 1879, Australian travel writer James Hingston published his popular book *The Australian Abroad*, through a respected London publisher. The book also describes the orchid mantis, but unlike Wallace, Hingston mistook the mantis for a carnivorous orchid:

After another cool night of sleep at Buitenzorg, I am taken by my kind host around his garden, and shown, among other things, a flower, a red orchid, that catches and feeds upon live flies. It seized upon a butterfly while I was present, and enclosed it in its pretty but deadly leaves, as a spider would have enveloped it in [its] network. The sensitive plant also grew here. Its leaves shrunk from a touch, and shrivelled up to nothing when plucked. That flower and this plant must have a nervous system closely allied to that of animals. The orchid to which I have referred has a delicate discrimination in the matter of its food. It must, in the fashion of an Eastern faith, kill its own meat – rejecting any dead fly that may fall upon its leaves.[7]

Hingston's book was popular and appears to have reached a significant audience. By writing in the first-hand travel writer's genre and simultaneously referencing the notorious 'sensitive plant' (*Mimosa pudica*), the author's voice would have carried a notable degree of authenticity, and certainly helped to spread the erroneous idea that orchids could be carnivorous.

The Flowering of the Strange Orchid

'The Flowering of the Strange Orchid', written by science fiction author H. G. Wells in 1894, was one of the earliest tales to describe killer orchids. The story tells of 'a shy, lonely, rather ineffectual man', Mr Winter-Wedderburn, whose sole passion is growing orchids.[8] He lives a very sedate life with his housekeeper (who, it is explained, is 'his remote cousin') and laments that he has such a dull life and that 'nothing ever happens' to him. Winter-Wedderburn longs for excitement, contrasting his boring life to that of the well-known orchid collector named Batten. Although Batten had recently been found dead in the tropical jungles, clutching a rare orchid plant, and 'every drop of blood' had been mysteriously drained from him, Winter-Wedderburn nevertheless envies his exhilarating legacy.[9]

One day, Winter-Wedderburn acquires a large assortment of orchids, including an exceedingly strange one that had been discovered

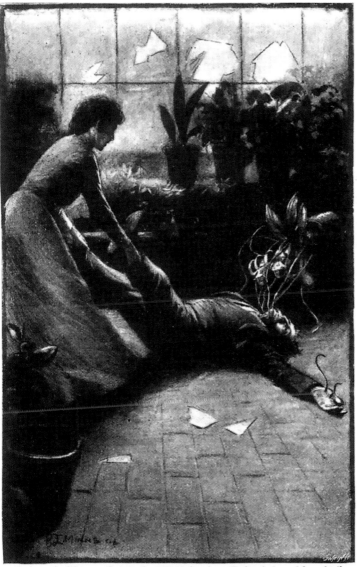

She tugged with renewed strength at Wedderburn's motionless body, and brought the strange orchid crashing to the floor.

Illustration by Frederick Henry Townsend, from H. G. Wells's
'The Flowering of the Strange Orchid' (1894).

by Batten on his last orchid-hunting expedition. Although Winter-Wedderburn is infatuated with the plant, his housekeeper is nonplussed, commenting on its 'ugly shape' and remarking that 'It looks like a spider shamming dead.'[10]

After months of caring for and coddling the new strange orchid plant, it finally blooms. Upon approaching the flower, Winter-Wedderburn is immediately overcome by an 'intensely sweet scent'. Soon the room begins to spin and he passes out. Sometime later, his housekeeper finds him:

> He was lying, face upward, at the foot of the strange orchid. The tentacle-like aerial rootlets no longer swayed freely in the air, but were crowded together, a tangle of grey ropes, and stretched tight, with their ends closely applied to his chin and neck and hands . . . she saw from one of the exultant tentacles upon his cheek there trickled a little thread of blood . . . she tried to pull him away from the leech-like suckers. She snapped two of these tentacles, and their sap dripped red.[11]

Finally, the housekeeper manages to free him, dragging him out into the open air. Although Winter-Wedderburn 'had lost a good deal of blood', he soon recovers. But, rather than begrudging the orchid, he, quite humorously, becomes 'bright and garrulous . . . in the glory of his strange adventure'.[12] It seems to be a reoccurring plot device, in which a rather insipid, orchid-obsessed character will dream of great adventure – but merely live it vicariously through others. In this case, Winter-Wedderburn was overjoyed to have experienced just a whiff of the dangers that he envisioned the real-life orchid hunters must experience.

Green Thoughts

Although Wells's 'The Flowering of the Strange Orchid' is by far the most famous early killer-orchid text, perhaps the most inventive themes can be found in John Collier's short story 'Green Thoughts', first published in *Harper's Magazine* in 1931. It is an oddly written story, in which the details and the complexity of the plant and human relationships are incrementally revealed. It is also extremely tactful in its use of language and requires a certain amount of reading between the lines and a deciphering of innuendo in order to grasp many of its sexual and botanical undertones. On the one hand, it is an absurdly fantastic tale, but on the other it does accentuate a number of themes that are specific to the orchid plant.

The story describes a mild-mannered orchid enthusiast named Mannering. One day he acquires a very strange orchid, and although *he* doesn't realize it at the time, the reader immediately understands its carnivorous tendencies. However, its carnivority is unique: rather than simply digesting its prey, the orchid more accurately *absorbs* them

GREEN THOUGHTS

by JOHN COLLIER

This title image for John Collier's 'Green Thoughts' (1931) features a 'carnivorous orchid' which absorbs its victims and subsequently produces a flower in the shape of their head. Illustration from *Shock* magazine (May 1960).

into its being. The victim then becomes visibly a part of the orchid as its ensuing flower will precisely mimic the appearance of the victim's head. Importantly, within this flower-head, the victim will still retain their own consciousness.

As would be expected in such a narrative, the orchid plant consumes increasingly larger victims. First, the orchid eats several flies – each one is then absorbed into the plant and becomes a tiny flower, and each of these flowers accurately mimics the shape and scale of a fly's head. When Mannering is compelled to leave town on business, his cousin Jane (who has a pet cat) agrees to look after his orchids. Things, of course, do not go well for the pair. Soon, the orchid consumes Cousin Jane's cat. Subsequently, a large flower appears, mimicking the exact shape and size of the cat's head. A few days later, Cousin Jane (who it is revealed is a part-time nudist) stands naked in front of the plant, shocked to see a flower in the shape of her beloved pet cat. As she stands there, stunned, she is slowly eaten. Soon, a giant flower appears that precisely mimics the head of Cousin Jane.

Upon returning home, and after having a shower, Mannering enters the greenhouse in only his loose-fitting bathrobe. He is shocked to see the new flowers – one that looks exactly like a cat's head and the other just like his Cousin Jane. As he stands there, in front of the unrelenting stares of the cat flower and the Cousin-Jane flower, he begins to feel self-conscious that he is wearing only a robe (which is only partially covering his nakedness). Mannering attempts to quickly adjust the robe, but it inadvertently falls to the ground. As he stands there naked, horrified and 'rooted to the spot', the orchid plant attacks him. A few days later, he also emerges as an orchid flower, yet retaining his human consciousness.

After a while, flower-Mannering becomes aware of a bee buzzing around his floral-head and, to his surprise, it enters his floral-mouth. His astonishment soon turns to mild pleasure as the bee collects his 'pollen' and then exits his floral-mouth. But to his shock and horror, he notices that the bee next pays a visit to the flower-head of Cousin

Jane. He suddenly realizes that he is about to have floral-sexual relations with her. As the bee enters Cousin Jane's floral-mouth, she also clearly realizes the implications of such a union, and is equally horrified.

Some weeks later, Mannering's nephew arrives to sort out the affairs of his missing (now presumed dead) uncle. He discovers the orchid flowers growing in the shape of his uncle and of Cousin Jane; and he also notices his uncle's bathrobe discarded on the ground. The nephew quickly realizes that it is a killer orchid, but also correctly surmises that he is safe from its power because he is fully clothed. He also concludes (incorrectly) that the two cousins had been involved in a relationship and they had, therefore, got what they deserved. To further add to this 'deserved' punishment, the nephew grabs a pair of scissors and swiftly decapitates his uncle's floral-head.

This story seems to reinforce the idea that those who are involved with orchids will undoubtedly suffer from some sort of depravity. In fact, Cousin Jane had 'always maintained that in the end no good would come of [Mannering's] preoccupation with those unnatural flowers'. And, at the conclusion of the story, when the lawyer is assisting with closing up Mannering's affairs, he divulges that he had also secretly wondered what fate might befall Mannering, due to his obsession with orchids; would it be 'Drugs? Sexual perversion? Or murder?'[13]

One of the obvious themes of this story is that orchids are extraordinary mimics. Most readers would have been aware of the common British and European bee orchids, whose flowers visibly mimic insect forms. This concept is, of course, increasingly amplified as each new victim is consumed and subsequently incorporated into the plant's form. Another idea touched upon is the unconventional manner in which orchids sexually reproduce. The idea of pseudo-copulation had recently been published in scientific journals, and of course Darwin's writings on cross-pollination were also well known. One might also wonder if the description of the self-crossed pollination between the two cousin flowers may be a veiled reference to

Darwin's real-life marriage to *his* cousin, and the subsequent disquiet that he felt regarding the potential genetic implications that this might have.

The final idea that comes across in this tale is a much subtler and more philosophical one, concerning how a plant and an insect could so dramatically cross the species barrier and engage in what we now refer to as pseudocopulation. That is, how could an animal become similar enough to a plant, or how could a plant become similar enough to an animal, for such a union to occur? Although Mannering's orchid plant is quite aggressive and is able to reach out its tendrils, leaves and aerial roots to grab and absorb its victims, it also requires them to, in a sense and in a way reminiscent of pseudocopulation, meet it halfway. In this case, the human must be entirely naked (and thus shed some of its civilized human identity). Second the naked human must remain motionless for several minutes and (like a plant) be 'rooted on the spot' so that the plant has time to grab and absorb the victim. The orchid must go to great pains to impersonate a female insect, but also the male insect is required to, in effect, change its mindset and cognitively blur what it actually sees before it with what it desires.

This story appears to have been liberally appropriated by several other writers. It formed the basis of a 1954 story in the American comic book series *The Monster of Frankenstein*, where the monster is compelled to bring larger and larger victims to a carnivorous plant. Likewise, after consuming its victim, the carnivorous plant produces growths that precisely mimic its victim's form. Similarly, Roger Corman's Hollywood B-movie *The Little Shop of Horrors* (1960), written by Charles B. Griffith, features a carnivorous plant named Audrey Jr which also displays flowers that mimic its victims.

Pokémon's Orchid

Deadly orchids continue to appear throughout popular culture, and a unique (and rather confusing) iteration can be found in the fictional realm of Pokémon (video games, animation series and card games). This particular Pokémon character (echoing the misinterpretations of the previously mentioned nineteenth-century travel writer James Hingston) seems to conflate the identities of an orchid mantis insect and an orchid flower.

The juvenile version of this Pokémon character is called Fomantis and it resembles a simple anthropomorphic orchid flower. In this state, it will frequently emit a pleasant aroma and will attract small insect characters known as 'Cutiflies' which engage in friendly and mutualistic relationships. However, when the Fomantis matures, it suddenly transforms into a killer orchid named Lurantis. In this adult form, Lurantis takes on the appearance of an orchid mantis. It uses its attractive colouring, design and orchid flower scent to lure a wide range of insects. Once these are within striking distance, it will aggressively attack using its razor-sharp 'petals'.[14]

What is most surprising about the adult character of the Lurantis Pokémon is that even though it looks more or less like an orchid mantis, it is still intended to be an orchid flower, thereby inverting the mimetic nature of the orchid and the mantis. Thus, rather than an orchid mantis mimicking an orchid flower (in order to attract its prey), the Lurantis is effectively a carnivorous orchid that takes on the form of an orchid mantis so as to become a more effective killer.

Adventurous Orchids

Orchids have had an extensive history of being associated with danger. This, of course, was fuelled by the fact that the most sought-after orchids were to be found in distant jungles in which there would be a number of potential perils (including dangerous animals, violent storms, diseases and local populations who might not appreciate trespassing foreigners). These dangers were often amplified and greatly exaggerated by successful orchid hunters who wished not only to build their reputation for bravery, but to discourage other hunters from marauding through their plunder sites.

Frederick Boyle, who had written numerous accounts of real-life orchid hunters, tried his hand at writing a fictional novel. He teamed up with co-writer Ashmore Russan and published *The Orchid Seekers: A Story of Adventure in Borneo* in 1897. Nearly four hundred pages in length, it details countless orchid-hunting adventures, although it does try to retain a plausible tone throughout most of its sprawling narrative.

Published a decade later, the 1910 short story 'The Black Orchid' by Marjorie L. C. Pickthall tells of an expedition team, consisting of Bob Warwick and Otto Mueller and their guide, Rosario, who set out into the jungles of the Amazon. They begin searching for the ruins of a temple, upon which a black orchid is said to grow. Mueller, however, is doubtful that it will be *truly* black – expecting that it will instead turn out to be merely a dark purple orchid. But Rosario insists that the orchid does exist, and that it is truly black. However, he does caution that it is divinely protected and that they must only look at it, and not touch or remove it. Eventually they find the elusive black orchid, and Mueller, ignoring Rosario's pleas, leaps up onto the stone platform. There, at the base of the great stone carving of the god, he grasps at the orchid. But the stone platform tilts under his feet and he is shot down into the darkness of a huge underground cavern. The stone door, which swings on a central pivot, slams shut. After a concerted effort, the rest of the team are eventually able to prise open the stone door and, with a rope, haul Mueller back to safety. Sadly, it is then revealed that 'The orchid was crushed to pulp by the upswing of the stone. There is nothing of it left. And it was the only one.'[15] Disheartened, the team head back home – never again to lay eyes upon a true black orchid. What is most interesting about this story is the detailed description of the tilting platform which propels Mueller into the cavern. This is an apt analogous description of the way many mobile orchids operate: their labellum will tilt forward and propel a visiting insect into the interior of the flower.

A number of these adventure tales stray into the realm of the supernatural. For example, the comic book story 'Slaves of the Orchid Goddess', from 1953, combines an orchid-hunting adventure story with a killer-orchid narrative. In this story, two co-owners of a 'smart florist shop in New York' venture into the jungles of Bangladesh and find a rare orchid which they plan to bring back to New York. One of the florists exclaims that 'If we can get it home and develop it we'll really have something!' The other florist is not so sure. Unfortunately, the orchid turns out to be carnivorous and is powerfully cursed by an orchid goddess. As a result, many New Yorkers suffer a gruesome fate.[16]

Echoes of early orchid-hunting adventures can be found in the Hollywood feature film *Anacondas: The Hunt for the Blood Orchid* (dir. Dwight H. Little, 2004). The film is infused with equal parts adventure and horror, as it depicts a group of explorers searching for a rare tropical orchid. In this case the explorers, who are funded by a large pharmaceutical company, travel to the jungles of Borneo in order to find a (fictional) rare orchid known as *Perrinnia immortalis*, or what is commonly known as 'the blood orchid'. It is believed that the flower of this orchid, which only blooms every seven years, can provide a 'fountain of youth', causing human and animal cells to live longer and persistently replicate. Upon entering the jungles where the orchid is reported to grow, they are soon attacked by enormous and vicious anacondas. It is later revealed that the reason these snakes grow to such enormous sizes is that they have eaten the flowers of 'the blood orchid' and therefore live much longer and never stop growing. Although it is clear that the greatest and most imminent terror that the explorers face is that of the giant attacking anacondas, these terrifying snake-monsters are in fact fuelled by the rare and mysterious orchid flower.

'Slaves of the Orchid Goddess', *Baffling Mysteries* (March 1953).

Orchid Superhero

There have been several different versions of the enigmatic super-hero character known simply as Black Orchid; each was created by a different publisher. Significantly, the character of Black Orchid is a female superhero and, unlike many other early female superheroes, she was not created as an afterthought patterned on an already existing male superhero (such as Supergirl, derived from Superman, and She Hulk, derived from the Hulk).

The earliest version of the Black Orchid superhero, Judy Allen, was introduced in 1943. A leading private investigator by day, she and her detective partner, Rocky Ford, work together to solve crimes. At night, however, Judy dons her disguise and becomes the Black Orchid.

She tells no one of her secret superhero identity, not even Ford, who, coincidentally, is also secretly a superhero, going by the name of Scarlet Nemesis. He also tells no one of his secret superhero identity. As a further remarkable coincidence, when appearing together as superheroes, Black Orchid and Scarlet Nemesis routinely team up to fight villains (just as they do during the day as ordinary detectives). Thus, they will set out 'for their nightly crusade against crime'; however, 'their identity [is] unknown to each other.' In addition to her fighting skills, the Black Orchid has an endless supply of daggers with black orchid flowers attached, which she wields and throws at her opponents.[17]

An early iteration of the superhero Black Orchid, published in the comic book *The Black Orchid* (1944). In this version, the superhero is more akin to a super detective.

The origin issue of a new iteration of Black Orchid, published in
DC's *Adventure Comics* series (1973). Black Orchid's purple costume and
her ability to fly make her, according to the other comic book characters, look
like a flying orchid. She is also, like an orchid, a master of disguise and mimicry.

The second version of the Black Orchid appeared the following year, in 1944, through a different independent publisher. This Black Orchid character is introduced as 'glamorous Diana Dawn, District Attorney Richard Day's secretary, who is – unknown to him – masquerading as the mysterious female sleuth the Black Orchid who solves crimes with the aid of a magic ring'. Her magic ring is purpose-built and can release 'paralyzing gases' which instantly knock out her opponents. Upon saving a victim, she presents them with a rare black orchid flower.[18]

In the 1970s, the American comic publisher DC introduced an ongoing series featuring a wholly new version of Black Orchid. Although most superheroes are shrouded in mystery, this version of the character is even more mysterious than most, as even the reader is unaware of Black Orchid's true identity.

In this series, Black Orchid is a much more modern superhero, but her mode of operation is, like her earlier versions, still primarily detective-driven. She researches her opponents thoroughly, learning everything there is to know about the criminals that she pursues. However, since no one knows her civilian identity – not even the reader – both the characters in the comic and the reader are continually misled as to what her true identity might be. The introduction to issue number two of the series states:

> She appears where there is evil, and is gone in a twinkling once it has been conquered! No one knows who she is, or from whence she acquired her extraordinary powers . . . she has the strength of a regiment, flies through the air like a bird of prey . . . and has the beauty and compassion of a young girl! Many have tried to guess her secrets, but all have failed.[19]

Compared to other superhero comics of the era, this version of Black Orchid exhibits a greater degree of sensitivity and nuance. She is careful and meticulous; she plans her attacks prudently and goes to great lengths to avoid hurting anyone. The manner in which she goes about apprehending the criminals is almost more important than whether she is successful. For example, in the midst of a battle she will stop a 'good character' from killing 'a criminal' by saying, 'I understand exactly how you feel, Sam Hendricks! But you are not a murderer!'[20] Not only does the Black Orchid seek to 'get the bad guys', she will go to great lengths to repair some of the social damage that may have transpired – such as helping the victims get their lives back together and restoring their tarnished reputations. Most significantly, being an orchid-themed hero, she is an incredible mimic and a master of disguise. She goes to great lengths to hide her identity and infiltrates criminal gangs. Often, after the criminals are thwarted, a rubber mask and wig will be found at the scene, revealing that the maid or the secretary had actually been Black Orchid in disguise. After leaving the scene she will frequently drop a black orchid, usually with a note attached. As she flies away, witnesses will invariably remark that she indeed does look like 'a flying black orchid!'[21]

In 1989 a new Black Orchid narrative, written by Neil Gaiman and illustrated by Dave McKean, emerged. In this version, the complexities of the superhero's floral roots are explored. It is revealed that Black Orchid is the result of early experiments by a botanist named Phil Sylvian who had 'dreamed of showing mankind that the world was one thing . . . all connected, intertwined'. The botanists hoped to 'make people of plants . . . breathing in carbon dioxide . . . breathing out oxygen . . . to create a new world . . . to save an old world from dying'.[22] Importantly, Black Orchid's unconventional approach is more fully explored in this series, as she not only fights crime but seeks to better understand who and what she is.

Orchids and Crime

One of the best-known characters associated with both crime and with orchids is private detective Nero Wolfe. Between 1934 and 1975, the author Rex Stout wrote over thirty novels and numerous short stories and novellas about this fictional detective, who happens to be

'Death Wears an Orchid', as it appeared in *The American Magazine* (1941). This Nero Wolfe story, written by Rex Stout, was later published in book form as *Black Orchids* (1942).

obsessed with collecting and growing orchids. Stout's Nero Wolfe stories have been adapted for radio and television, and a number of other authors have penned further stories based on Stout's original characters. Wolfe is a brilliant detective and a very large man (weighing over 130 kilograms (300 lb)). He rarely leaves his home; instead,

155

his assistant Archie Goodwin does most of the legwork, while Wolfe does most of the thinking and actual solving of the crimes.

Nero Wolfe, according to the 1942 novella *Black Orchids*, has over 20,000 orchids in his collection.[23] In this story, the one variety that seems to be missing from his collection is a 'black orchid' Upon hearing that one is to be exhibited at the upcoming annual orchid show, Wolfe sends Goodwin to investigate and report back to him whether it is truly black or not. In predictable fashion, a murder takes place at the flower show. After Wolfe is hired to solve the case, he soon determines that the murder was the result of a rivalry between two plant growers – something akin to extreme 'horticultural jealousy'. As payment for his detective services, Wolfe is given the three black orchids that were on display at the show. Sometime later, as he proudly displays the orchids on his desk, Police Commissioner Cramer drops by to congratulate him. The commissioner politely agrees that the flowers are 'pretty', but reckons they are 'Kind of drab, though. Not much color,' adding (much to Wolfe's horror) that he 'likes geraniums better'.[24] The reader, of course, knowing Nero Wolfe's obsession with orchids, would understand that this was perhaps the worst insult that one could hurl at him.

In another story, 'The Bashful Body' (dramatized as a radio play in 1950), a body is discovered at a local flower shop. When Wolfe learns that the body was found in among a display of lilies, he refuses to investigate, stating that 'Anyone who would permit himself to be found dead or alive among a display of lilies is beneath contempt.' But then when he learns that the murder victim was an eminent orchid grower, he quickly changes his mind and agrees to take the case.

Not all of the Nero Wolfe plotlines are centred on orchids, but they are always to be found somewhere in the story. Wolfe will spend many hours each day tending to his orchids; he will carefully read all of the latest scientific journal articles pertaining to orchids and he will, on occasion, publish articles himself. Frequently, his detective work takes second place to his orchid obsession. Nero Wolfe stories continue to be popular today, and over the decades they have played at least a small role in popularizing the growing of orchids. Some orchid enthusiasts have even attributed their initial interest in orchids to Nero Wolfe. A number of orchid hybrids have been named after the character.

Orchids and crime also figure in the classic British film *Black Orchid* (Charles Saunders, 1953), which describes a tale of 'love gone wrong', the titular flower becoming the pivotal clue that is used to uncover the true identity of the murderer. The film introduces an unhappily married couple, Dr John Winnington and Sophie Winnington. Within a few weeks, Sophie Winnington is murdered, being poisoned by nicotine. Initially the husband is blamed; however, it is later revealed that the actual murderer is Eric Blair, an obsessive orchid grower. It seems that Blair had spent over ten years developing his pure black orchid (a black *Cypripedium*), claimed to be the only one in the world. Sophie Winnington wore a black orchid the night she died and, as a result, it is ultimately proven that Eric Blair was the murderer. Although orchids play only a small part in the overall narrative, the film does seem to imply that there is something inherently suspect about orchid growers. Anyone who would spend ten years secretly developing a black orchid would no doubt be capable of – or perhaps even prone to – committing a violent murder.

The popular hero James Bond also becomes entangled in a narrative of orchids and crime. In the movie *Moonraker* (dir. Lewis Gilbert, 1979), Bond must face off against the villain known as Hugo Drax, who is intent on taking over the world. Drax devises an evil plan which he dubs 'Operation Orchid' involving the use of a rare (fictional) orchid, *Orchidae nigra* (which, not surprisingly, translates as 'black orchid'). Drax menacingly explains to Bond that the orchid is sacred to an Indigenous people of the Amazon; its pollen, after extensive exposure, causes sterility in humans. Drax claims that he has 'improved' on this side effect through experimentation at his secret research lab: he has successfully derived a deadly nerve gas from the orchid. When Bond confronts him, Drax launches into a rambling tirade:

The curse of a civilization! It was neither war nor pestilence that wiped out the race who built the great city lying around us. It was their reverence for this lovely flower. Because long-term exposure to its pollen caused sterility. Correct, Mr. Bond. As you discovered, I have improved upon sterility. Those same seeds now yield death!

Drax then clarifies that his orchid weapon does not kill 'animals or plant life', quipping, 'One must preserve the balance of nature.' Although Drax's plan is absurdly nonsensical, he does fit the well-established character type of the 'evil horticulturalist', who tends to place plant life above human life.

The long-running science fiction television series *Doctor Who* devoted a two-part episode (originally broadcast in 1982) to the mysteries of a black orchid. In the eponymous episode, the Doctor and his three travelling companions find themselves in 1920s England. Other than their arrival from another time and place, this episode plays out like a standard whodunnit murder mystery. It also, somewhat tenuously, echoes the orchid-like theme of mimicry. The Doctor and his companion, Nyssa, are initially mistaken for two other people and are subsequently invited to a fancy-dress party at a large estate. They arrive to find the guests all admiring a large black orchid on prominent display. Before long, a murder takes place. Initially, the Doctor is accused as he had chosen to wear the same harlequin costume that is also worn by the real murderer. It turns out that the actual murderer is George Cranleigh, the famous botanist and explorer. As a rationalization for his murderous ways, it is explained that Cranleigh had collected a rare black orchid while in Brazil. But as it was a sacred flower to the local people, 'they cut out his tongue and his mind was affected.' Later, as the Doctor and his companions leave the party, they are presented with a gift. It is a book, written by George Cranleigh some ten years earlier and simply titled *Black Orchid*.

The American daily newspaper comic strip *Brenda Starr, Reporter* was created by female cartoonist Dale Messick. It was enormously

The cover of this 1963 comic book features the investigative journalist Brenda Starr with her mysterious love interest Basil St John. Note the large black orchid in the foreground, which St John uses to create a serum to prevent him from 'going mad'.

popular and ran continuously for seventy years (from 1940 to 2011) in newspapers around the world. It was also made into a comic book series, a theatrical film serial, as well as a live-action feature film starring Brooke Shields (1992). Brenda Starr is presented as a fearless newspaper reporter, who frequently becomes entangled in mysterious and dangerous adventures as she pursues her investigations. In among these journalistic endeavours, she has an ongoing love interest, a mysterious man named Basil St John. He wears a black eyepatch and frequently sends her black orchids in order to show his affection and signal that he has returned from one of his lengthy journeys abroad. In one sequence, it is revealed that St John collects these rare black orchids in order to

> extract a serum, which is the only remedy known that will prevent all the male members of the St. John family from going mad! Since black orchids are rare, they only grow in the densest regions of the Amazon jungle, the supply is extremely limited – so until [Basil St John] discovers a way to grow black orchids in civilized countries – he comes and goes in Brenda's life, here today – gone tomorrow – depending on the supply of black orchid serum![25]

In the final newspaper strip (published Sunday, 2 January 2011), Brenda Starr receives a delivery, and inside the box is a black orchid, accompanied by a card inscribed simply with the initials 'BSJ'. The card, of course, refers to her enduring love interest, Basil St John, who has presumably just returned from another mysterious overseas expedition.

The Orchid Thief and Adaptation

The year 1998 marked the publication of Susan Orlean's non-fiction book The Orchid Thief. Based on true events, it begins by recounting the details of a court case in Florida, involving plant poachers and

Adaptation (2002, dir. Spike Jonze), based on Susan Orlean, *The Orchid Thief* (1998). Here, the character John Laroche admires an orchid display, including the much sought-after ghost orchid (*Dendrophylax lindenii*), while the character of Susan Orlean (Meryl Streep) looks on.

the removal of protected orchid plants (particularly the ghost orchid, *Dendrophylax lindenii*) from the swamplands of Florida. It also describes the life and obsessions of the central 'orchid thief', John Laroche, as well as the quest by the author (Susan Orlean) to attempt to understand the strange world of orchids and their passionate enthusiasts. The book also, as it details the illegal but lucrative trade in orchids, further underscores the correlation between crime and orchids. *The Orchid Thief* is unconventional in its sprawling style, and defied all expectations by rapidly becoming a best-seller.

Even more surprisingly, just four years later, the book was made into the feature film *Adaptation* (2002), written by Charlie Kaufman, directed by Spike Jonze and starring Nicolas Cage and Meryl Streep. What makes the film so intriguing is that the very process of adapting the unconventional book into a screenplay becomes a significant part of the narrative. The emphasis of the film, therefore, is on the screenwriter struggling with how he is going to adapt the 'sprawling' subject-matter of *The Orchid Thief* into a Hollywood film.

On closer reading, a number of orchid-related themes also emerge, such as identity and the evolutionary process by which orchids have adapted to entice their pollinators. This plays out as Charlie Kaufman (Nicolas Cage) struggles to 'adapt' the book into an innovative and unconventional work of filmic art. In the film's narrative, the screenwriter's identity (and his desire to create a sensitive piece about orchids and those that cultivate them) is compromised in the process when his twin brother takes over the screenwriting project. As a result, the final thirty minutes of the film (in a self-reflexive and darkly humorous manner) becomes a clichéd Hollywood blockbuster full of car chases, drugs, murders and dangerous animals.

Similarly, the idea that someone might be totally enamoured with orchids simply because of their beauty and their singularity is also compromised, and supplanted with a crasser Hollywood justification. Thus, it is revealed that people are actually obsessed with the

The flower of the ghost orchid, a leafless epiphytic orchid which conducts photosynthesis through its roots.

(fictional) ghost orchid not because of its beauty, but because it contains a powerful mind-altering drug. Subsequently, the fictionalized character of author Susan Orlean (Meryl Streep) learns of the orchid's drug and soon develops an addiction to it. Ultimately the film *Adaptation* takes a darkly humorous look at Hollywood films, the screenwriting process and the process of adapting literature into film. However, it still manages to consider and highlight the intriguing world of orchids.

Orchids of Distinction

During the 'golden age' of orchid popular culture (late nineteenth and early twentieth centuries) orchids were extremely expensive. Often they became the organic equivalent of diamonds and rubies for the rich and famous. In the midst of this era, a significant British statesman and politician who was a recognized orchid enthusiast, Joseph Chamberlain (1836–1914), emerged. Chamberlain became known for his ever-present monocle and his trademark orchid, which he wore on his lapel.

It is said that Joseph Chamberlain was a rather nondescript person who wore his signature monocle, and in particular his showy orchids, in order to stand out. Conversely, when he once travelled on a sea voyage on HMS *Good Hope*, he strove to blend in with the other passengers. According to a 1902 article in *Punch* magazine it did not take much effort for him to go incognito: 'He had disguised himself by removing his eye-glass and orchid, and, when found, was engaged in conversation with some of the engineers who, on learning that their visitor was the Colonial Secretary, were amazed at the intelligence of the questions he put to them.'[26] In fact, he became so well known for the orchid on his lapel and his interest in growing orchids that he was sometimes caricatured simply as an anthropomorphized orchid. After his death in 1914, several of his orchid houses were used as convalescent centres for British soldiers wounded in the First World War.

Caricature of British
politician Joseph
Chamberlain, who
regularly wore a
monocle and an
orchid flower pinned
to his lapel. In this
postcard from 1903
he appears as an
anthropomorphized
orchid flower.

THE POLITICAL ORCHID,
"RESIGNATION"

The Wrench Series, No. 10478   (Copyright)

Orchids also took centre stage in the 1903 British musical comedy
The Orchid. The stage show featured romance and comedic drama
and involved the quest for a rare Peruvian orchid. In the end, the
orchid hunters never do find the elusive flower, but to everyone's surprise they discover a very similar orchid species growing at the local
horticultural college in London. The discovery of this home-grown
orchid serves as a metaphor, encouraging one to find provincial love
and discouraging the pursuit of the exotic and, by extension, marry-
ing beyond one's own position. The show was very popular and was
attended by several members of the British royal family. In fact, over
the years, the royal family has included a number of orchid enthusiasts,
such as, most notably, Queen Victoria. Having such prominent devo-
tees would certainly have elevated the orchid's status even further.

Another public figure who became synonymous with orchids was Georges Carpentier (1894–1975). Carpentier was a French world champion boxer who enjoyed international acclaim during a career that lasted from 1908 to 1926. Although he was an outstandingly talented boxer and won a number of championships, it was his persona and decorum that ultimately made him so famous. In America, he was nicknamed 'The Orchid Man' and was renowned for his 'debonair good looks and suave charm', which contrasted greatly with the 'brutish' reputation of other boxers of the era. After retiring from boxing, he became an actor, an investor and finally opened up the first cocktail bar in Paris.[27] His nickname remained with him, and a popular perfume called 'The Orchid Man' was named after him. The perfume, produced by P. Frapin & Cie, is still available today, and one Australian distributor describes it as a 'sweet, spicy scent [that] perfectly reflects the man it was inspired by . . . A man who can definitely look after himself, but also scrubs up alright & will take you out dancing after he's won the fight.'[28]

Speaking of Orchids

In America, during the latter part of the nineteenth century and the early twentieth century, the phrase 'orchids and turnips' was part of the popular lexicon. Since orchids were, by then, regarded as the most exclusive of flowers, the phrase would be playfully used to differentiate between important people (the 'orchids') and common people (the 'turnips'). It is believed that the phrase was derived from the French expression 'les grosses et les petites legumes' meaning 'big vegetables' (important people) and 'small vegetables' (common people).

In the 1930s, Walter Winchell, an American newspaper columnist and radio commentator, updated the 'orchids and turnips' expression to 'orchids and scallions'. Orchids were more popular than ever at the time and their allure and positive association were obvious. In contrast, a 'scallion' (a spring onion or shallot) has not only a very pungent odour but suggests the derogatory term of 'scallywag'. In Winchell's newspaper column and weekly radio show, he would comment on the politicians and socialites of the day – awarding 'orchids' to those worthy of praise and 'scallions' to those worthy of censure. Winchell's commentaries had a great impact on American society, and as one article noted, 'His unique gibberish, unintelligible to readers a decade ago, today forms the basis of a national slanguage. His chatter is on every tongue.'[29] Many other writers and publications appropriated Winchell's terms and would bestow their own 'orchids' and 'scallions'.

From this terminology, the simple phrase 'orchids to you' soon became a common American expression of congratulations or approval. In stark contrast, in British slang, 'orchids to you' became a euphemism for the more vulgar 'bollocks to you' or 'balls to you' (owing to the testicular shape of many terrestrial orchid tubers).

Orchids in Advertising

In American advertising, the word 'orchid' began to be used as a way of describing the best of something. For example: 'the orchids of home appliances' would suggest the very best in appliances. This usage became widespread as well as varied. For example, a car tyre advertisement from 1919 declared, 'What Orchids are to flowers, Silvertown Cords are to tires. Most graceful, most distinctive.' A print advertisement from the 1930s, promoting Hickory Perma-Lift Brassieres, used the slogan, 'You'll say "an orchid to the lift that never lets you down".' And 'Orchids to your dream . . .' was the slogan used in a 1940s advertisement to prompt readers to purchase the 'petal-smooth beauty of Dan River sheets'.

As orchids gained a reputation for being the most precious of flowers, they also became the standard against which other things were judged (similar to how gold, the most precious of metals, can be described as the 'gold standard'). For example, an advertisement from 1921 for Paul's berry jams declared, 'The berry is the orchid of the fruits. In delicacy of flavors it can be compared only to the colors

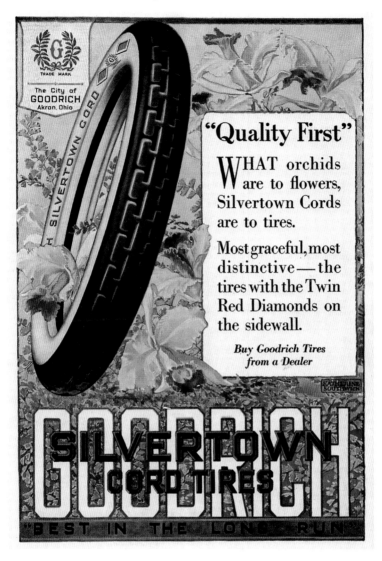

American print advertisement from 1919, using orchids to promote automobile tyres.

of the orchid.' Likewise, a 1937 advertisement for canned Green Giant Peas proclaimed that theirs were 'The Orchid of the Pea Family'.

Other advertisements used orchids to establish a product's value or exclusive nature. A 1949 advertisement for Harry and David's mail order gift packages promised, 'This Christmas you can give

"Orchid" gifts at "Daisy" prices!' Similarly, a 1946 ad for Chrysler cars stated, 'They go well together . . . orchids and the Chrysler Town and Country . . . perfect background for those to whom distinction comes naturally.'

As air travel became more accessible, while still being seen as a glamorous undertaking, advertisements for Western Airlines not

Odontoglossum crispum, from *Lindenia* (1887), vol. III.

This advertising card from *c.* 1897 depicts an anthropomorphized orchid and cactus flower. In South American jungles, it is common to find an epiphytic cactus (commonly referred to as the orchid cactus) growing alongside epiphytic orchids.

only utilized orchids to elevate the status of their company but offered orchid flowers as premiums to their customers. One of their advertisements from 1957 depicts a stewardess presenting an orchid to a female traveller. The recipient appears enthralled, while her husband, standing behind her, is even more pleased to see her beguilement. The ad states, 'Lovely orchids add the finishing touch to a delightful travel experience. Just one of the little extras – at no extra fare – that have made Western's celebrated "Champagne Flights" America's smartest air service!' And of course, increased air travel also made overseas tourism more accessible and soon the orchid had become a symbol of many tropical destinations, including Venezuela, Hawai'i and Singapore.

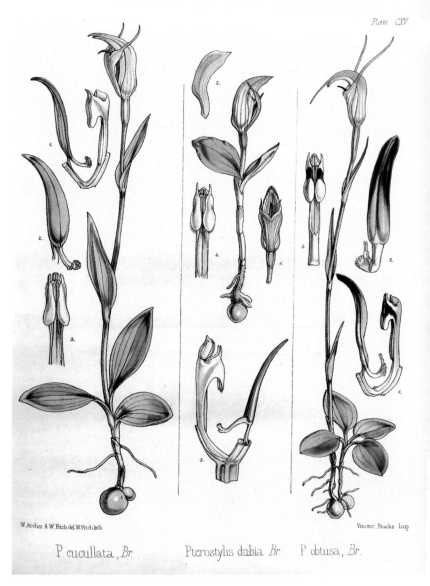

Plate CXV

W. Archer & W. Fitch del W. Fitch lith.

Vincent Brooks Imp.

P. cucullata, *Br.*   Pterostylis dubia *Br.*   P. obtusa, *Br.*

Pterostylis nutans, or nodding greenhood orchids. The tubers of these orchids
were just some of many species that served as a traditional food source
for several Indigenous groups in Australia.

six
Consuming Orchids
ᘒ

H umans have been consuming orchids for thousands of years – and we continue to do so on a considerable scale. Across the world, orchids are used as food, flavouring, fragrances and medicine. The dried 'fruits' from vanilla orchids are used extensively in flavouring, perfumes and other scented products. Orchid tubers, leaves and flowers have also provided nourishment to many. A wide range of species are also used in traditional medicines, and in a few cases are playing a promising role in contemporary medical research.

Consuming Orchid Tubers

Nowhere has the consumption of orchid tubers been more significant and more enduring than on the Australian continent, where terrestrial orchids once carpeted much of the landscape. The Indigenous peoples of Australia, who make up the oldest continuous civilizations in the world, extending back some 60,000 years, are believed to have incorporated orchids into their diets for much of this time. It is estimated that at least two hundred different species of orchid were consumed at one time or another.[1] In many instances, these orchids were sustainably managed. For example, when harvesting, only intermittent orchids would be dug up, creating spaces between existing plants and encouraging natural vegetative propagation. This is said to have amounted to a 'systematic and repetitive tilling process' which effectively 'aerated the soil, loosened it for seed germination and root penetration, and incorporated ash and compost material with the plants'.[2] One of the most commonly eaten species (particularly in southeastern Australia) has been the leafless bell orchid (*Gastrodia sesamoides*), also known as the potato orchid, as it produces a sweet-potato-sized tuber up to 15 centimetres (6 in.) long and 4 centimetres (1½ in.) in diameter.[3] Other popular tubers include the leopard orchids (*Diuris pardina*) and nodding greenhoods (*Pterostylis nutans*). Each of these tubers can be eaten either raw or cooked and their flavours have been described (depending on the species) as either 'starchy', 'watery', 'bitter' or 'sweet'.[4]

Upon arriving on the Australian continent, European colonists also learned to eat these prevalent orchid tubers. Writing in the 1800s, botanist J. Maiden wrote, 'There is hardly a country boy who has not eaten so-called Yams, which are the tubers of numerous kinds of terrestrial or ground-growing orchids.'[5] However, as more Europeans arrived, native orchid habitats were severely impacted. Wide-scale land clearing, and subsequent sheep and cattle grazing, destroyed many of the terrestrial orchid populations. Not only did these imported animals eat much of the natural vegetation, they altered the land and soil. Prior to this intense agricultural grazing activity, the soil was reported to have exhibited very unusual qualities. European settlers noted how the soil on the open plains was extremely 'friable' and the ground was covered in layers of moss and lichen that were so thick that when horses walked across they would sink 'to the fetlock in the soil as if it were sponge'.[6] Over the decades, the trampling hooves of the sheep and cattle significantly compacted the soil and ultimately destroyed the thick layers of moss and lichen that had served as an ideal growing medium for the orchids.

There was another unfortunate event (and one utterly staggering in its scope) which further decimated many native orchid populations, and that was the introduction of the European wild rabbit to the continent. In 1859, wealthy landowner Thomas Austin received a shipment of thirteen wild European rabbits from a relative in England.

He released these onto his estate (situated just outside Melbourne) so that he and his guests would have easy and familiar game to hunt. Needless to say, several of these rabbits got safely away, and within just sixty years they had spread to more than two-thirds of the Australian continent. By the 1920s it is estimated that there were a staggering 10 billion feral rabbits roaming across Australia.[7] These rabbits (along with the vast, growing numbers of grazing livestock) effectively decimated native vegetation, including the numbers and diversity of terrestrial orchids.

Terrestrial orchid tubers form part of a long history of sustenance in many other parts of the world. In Africa, a wide range of tubers have been eaten (either roasted or raw), including *Eulophia* spp. and *Satyrium* spp. In the Americas, too, orchid tubers were regularly consumed, including *Calypso borealis* and *Habenaria dilatata*, which would be eaten either raw, roasted or boiled. Raw, steamed or boiled tubers of a number of species were also frequently eaten in parts of India, China and Japan.[8]

Salep

Orchid tubers have also been widely consumed across Europe and West Asia. Their plentiful distribution provided an opportune and supplemental food for many. However, some 2,000 years ago, when the so-called Doctrine of Signatures came into vogue, Europeans' attitudes towards these orchid tubers dramatically changed.

In very broad terms, the Doctrine of Signatures described how different medicinal plants could be used, based on the parts of the human body they resembled. As many orchid tubers were thought to resemble testicles, they were summarily imbued with the false belief that they would have an invigorating and aphrodisiac effect on humans. The Greek philosopher and botanist Theophrastus was one of the earliest advocates for this use of orchid tubers. Writing in about 300 BCE he explained:

Firstly the physical effects, by which I mean favouring or inhibiting procreation. There is at least one plant whose root is said to show both powers. This is the [orchid], which has a double bulb, one large and one small. The larger, given in the milk of a mountain goat, produces more vigour in sexual intercourse; the smaller inhibits and forestalls . . . It is odd, certainly, that both powers should be found in the same plant; but that a plant should have one or other power need not surprise us.[9]

The claim of orchids as being aphrodisiacs and stimulants was given further credence when it was included in the *Herball of Dioscorides* (Pedanius Dioscorides, 40–90 CE). These claims were then extended into the Arab world (and subsequently to India) through the writings of the Persian physician and philosopher Ibn Sina (known to the West as Avicenna, 980–1037). The orchid's reputation as an aphrodisiac persisted for centuries and was recounted in subsequent European herbals, such as John Gerard's (published in 1597), which claimed that the tubers 'stir up venery'. As recently as the 1814 edition of Culpeper's *Herbal*, it was reiterated that orchid tubers are 'hot and moist in operation, under the dominion of Dame Venus, and provoke lust exceedingly, which, they say, the dried and withered roots do restrain'.[10] Numerous additional medicinal claims were made for these tubers – ranging from being able to eradicate worms from children to the successful treatment of tuberculosis. Orchid tubers were also heralded as being extremely nutritious, particularly for invalids and those in a weakened state;[11] in fact, many had come to believe that orchid tubers were practically a supernatural superfood.

It was against this backdrop that the salep food-craze emerged and quickly became a near worldwide phenomenon. Salep is the name given to the dried tubers of terrestrial orchids; it also refers to the powder prepared from these dried tubers and to the popular beverages and foods made from this orchid tuber powder. The term 'salep' is actually derived from the Arabic word *sahlab*, which comes

A traditional Turkish salep beverage vendor. This illustration was published in a French travel book from 1822.

from a colloquial term for 'fox'. Similar to the English, various species of terrestrial orchids were commonly referred to as dog's stones (dog testicles) or fox's stones (fox testicles). In Arabic, the most common orchids were known as fox's testicles (*khasyu alsahlab*), or simply fox (*alsahlab*). Over time, the powder and the beverage made from these orchids would be referred to by the abbreviated term *sahlab*. As a food and beverage, *sahlab* primarily came into vogue during the Ottoman Empire in what are now the regions of Turkey, Iran and Syria. By the sixteenth century *sahlab* had become exceedingly popular, particularly as a hot beverage, and could be purchased from most street vendors and cafés. It was soon exported to many other parts of the world, with Turkey being the main supplier.

When *sahlab* was exported to India it became known locally as *salam*. The imported *salam* would be divided into different classes, depending upon which type of orchid it had come from. If the originating tubers were round or oval in shape, the *salam* was called *salam mishri*; if the originating tubers were shaped like a human hand, it would be called *salam panja*.[12] When exported to Europe it became known by the more Westernized name salep (in Greece it is called *salepi*). When it reached the shores of Britain in the 1600s it eventually became known as 'saloop'. Salep was also consumed in North America, though very little of this was imported from Turkey; instead it was obtained from domestic orchids, such as *Habenaria*.[13] Today, salep is by far the most common and universal name for orchid tuber powder.

Customers enjoying British salep, known as 'saloop', in this illustration by Thomas Rowlandson, published in the 1820 collection *Rowlandson's Characteristic Sketches of the Lower Orders*.

Salep's popularity soon spread across Europe, and by the late 1600s it had become hugely popular in England, where it would be sold as a hot beverage by countless street vendors. The cry of 'Saloop! Loop! Loop!' could be heard echoing through the streets of London, particularly in the early morning hours. Not only was saloop an inexpensive and warming drink on chilly mornings, it gained the reputation for being extremely nutritious, and was considered to be an antidote for drunkenness. Hence, it was popular with late-night revellers on their way home, and with early-morning labourers who sought a nutritious and comforting drink to start their day.

Salep (or saloop) had several outspoken advocates in Britain, who championed its supposed nutritious qualities. In the early 1700s, prominent ship's surgeon James Lind claimed that '2 lb of salep and 2 lb portable soup [dried meat broth] will afford a wholesome diet to one person for a month because they contain the greatest quantity of vegetable and animal nourishment that can be reduced into so small a bulk.'[14] Sailors were instructed to combine 1 ounce (28 g) of salep powder and 1 ounce of portable soup (dried meat broth) with 2 quarts (2 l) of boiling water, which was deemed 'sufficient for a man a-day'.[15] Because of these highly inflated claims, virtually every British sailing ship that set sail over the next hundred years would carry large stores of portable soup and of salep.

Most of the salep powder used in Europe was imported from Turkey, but there were also those who sought to establish a local British salep industry. In 1768, J. Moult discovered how to produce salep powder using wild British orchids, such as *Orchis mascula*, and published an article on the subject:

> The best time to gather the roots is when the seed is formed, and the stalk going to fall, for then the new bulb, of which the Salep is made, is arrived to its full size . . . This new root, being separated from the stalk, is to be washed in water, and a fine thin skin, that covers it, to be taken off with a small brush; or, by dipping in hot water, it will come off with a

coarse linen cloth. When a sufficient quantity of the roots is thus cleaned, they are to be spread on a tin plate, and set into an oven, heated to the degree of a bread-oven, where they are to remain six, eight, or ten minutes, and have acquired a transparency like that of horn, but without being diminished in size. When they are arrived at this state, they may be removed to another room to dry and harden, which will be done in a few days; or they may be finished in a very slow heat, in a few hours. I have tried both ways with success.[16]

Moult concluded his article with a plea to Britons to begin farming orchids on a wide scale, saying, 'I hope it will encourage the cultivation of so nutritious a vegetable, so as to reduce it from its present high price . . . to one of moderate as would bring it into common use.'[17] Although Moult and others did begin to produce some quantities of British-made salep, the majority of it continued to be imported from Turkey.

Several British cookery books from the early 1800s provided variant recipes for making home-made salep. One suggested, 'Boil some wine, water, sugar, and lemon-peel, together; then add the saloop powder . . . and boil the whole a few minutes.'[18] Another advised, 'Take a large tea-spoonful of the powder of saloop, and put it into a pint of boiling water. Keep stirring it till it is a fine jelly; then add some wine and sugar.'[19]

British consumption of salep virtually disappeared by the mid-1800s, salep being replaced by tea and coffee as the predominate hot drinks. By the late 1800s it had become clear that 'salep possesses no medicinal powers' and even its reputation as being 'highly nutritious' was described as being merely an erroneous 'popular notion'.[20] However, the notion of salep did persist in British slang for some time. According to the 1913 edition of *The British Slang Dictionary*, the word 'slops' refers to a 'weak warm drink'; and the word 'slops' is thought to be derived from the Cockney pronunciation of saloop.[21]

Despite the patently false medicinal claims made for it, salep was found to offer some unique qualities as a culinary ingredient: it has the ability to thicken and remain transparent when added to hot liquids, and it can impart a novel elastic stretchiness to chilled liquids. Salep powder is used in a number of ways, but is most commonly added to boiling water or milk and gently flavoured with additional spices and sugar and served as a hot beverage. In Turkey, it was traditionally sold by street vendors from large brass urns which kept the beverage hot. It also began to be incorporated into desserts. For example, it would sometimes be added to halva (a popular sweet made of sesame and honey) and incorporated into breads or yogurts. It also was made into a sweet tapioca-like pudding. During the summer months, it would be prepared as a cold beverage.

Salep can also be added to ice cream. Salep ice cream, or *salepi dondurma* as it is known in Turkey, consists of three main ingredients: goat's milk, sugar and salep powder. Because of the added salep, it behaves very differently to normal ice cream: its consistency is thick, like dough, it is very chewy and stretchy and, most remarkably, it does not melt at room temperature. These attributes are due entirely to

Traditional Turkish ice cream (*salepi dondurma*). The inclusion of salep gives this ice cream a very firm and elastic consistency, as well as making it resistant to melting.

179

the inclusion of the salep powder and are amplified by laborious hand-churning of the chilled ice cream with long wooden or metal poles, to build up its elastic consistency.

In recent times, the making and selling of salep ice cream has become a very theatrical performance. Traditional Turkish ice-cream vendors are known as *salepçi*, and they will frequently dress in the traditional clothing of colourful vests, baggy trousers and striped cummerbunds. These *salepçi* will go to great lengths to showcase the ice cream's unusual elasticity, and in doing so will perform an array of entertaining tricks. This normally involves gently taunting the customer before they are finally given their ice cream in a cone. And, if a large crowd is gathered, these antics may persist for several minutes – compelling the customer to work very hard for their ice cream. For example, the *salepçi* might ask the customer to hold out an empty ice-cream cone, and then they will, much to the customer's surprise, momentarily place an enormous blob of ice cream (stuck on the end of a long pole) onto the top of the cone. Then, they will quickly pull the ice cream away, taking the cone with it, and leaving the customer empty-handed. Their theatrics are so pronounced that the occupational name of *salepçi* has now become Turkish slang for 'mischief maker'.[22]

Salep ice cream is available throughout Turkey, but the city of Kahramanmaras (located in the region of Marash) is known as the country's ice-cream capital and the origin centre of salep ice cream. Today, this ice cream is also widely consumed in several other countries, including Iran, Egypt, Syria and Greece. In Iran, salep ice cream is sometimes referred to as 'Akbar Mashdi' after the man who first produced it commercially there in the 1950s; while in Syria it is known as *buza*.[23] In the Greek city of Thessaloniki, salep ice cream is also widely available.

Historically, the worldwide consumption of salep was immense. At the peak of its popularity in the 1700s, it is claimed that the amount of salep powder exported to England alone (mostly from Turkey) was approximately 642,500 kilograms (101,200 st) each year.[24] Since it takes approximately 220–250 orchid tubers to produce 1 kilogram (2 lb) of salep powder, at a conservative estimate it would mean that over 141 million wild-harvested orchid tubers were imported to England each year.[25]

Today, salep (and salep ice cream) is still widely sold and consumed in some regions – and even appears to be gaining in popularity in recent years. This continues to put immense pressure on wild orchid populations as many millions of tubers are harvested each year. Some sustainable (cultivated) orchids are beginning to be used in salep production, but even when this is declared on the label, it is nearly always an unverifiable claim.[26] Fortunately, the majority of commercially available salep drink is now made with substitute ingredients, usually corn starch and guar gum, and therefore contains little or no actual orchid ingredients.

Writer Holly Chase, following her extensive research into Turkish cuisine, notes that there is 'no discernible difference in taste or mouth-feel between hot salep made with the precious powdered orchid root and faux salep made with cornstarch, the cheapest substitute'. She has described the following recipe for an orchid-free 'salep' drink:

2 tbs. cornstarch
[salep powder substitute]
4 cups milk (whole or reduced fat, but not skim)
3 tbs. granulated sugar, or more to taste
1 tsp vanilla extract
ground cinnamon

Stir 5 or 6 tablespoons of the milk into the cornstarch to make a smooth paste. Set bowl aside. In a saucepan, bring the remaining milk, uncovered, to a boil. Just as it begins to boil, reduce heat to low. Stir in the sugar and pour in the starch mixture, stirring vigorously, so that lumps do not form. Cook over very low heat, stirring continuously, until the milk thickens, about 8–10 minutes. Remove mixture from heat. Stir in vanilla extract. Serve salep in cups or mugs and dust each with cinnamon.[27]

Chikanda

An increasingly popular food in the southern African nations of Zambia, Tanzania and Malawi is known as *chikanda*.[28] This food is made from a variety of native terrestrial orchid tubers such as those of the genera *Disa*, *Habenaria* and *Satyrium*. The most common way to prepare *chikanda* involves mashing the tubers into a fine meal which is then dried. The resulting orchid tuber meal is then blended with nut meal, salt, bicarbonate of soda and chilli powder and added to boiling water to make a thick mixture. After cooling, the resulting *chikanda* is cut up into cubes or wedges and served.[29]

Recently the demand for *chikanda* has greatly increased. It is no longer regarded as a last-resort foodstuff, but is an increasingly

Chikanda, a traditional dish in Zambia that has risen in popularity in recent years. These cubed pieces are made from a cooked blend of orchid tubers and peanut meal.

Freshly peeled orchid tubers for sale at an open market in Mbeya, Tanzania.

sought-after cuisine that is sold in high-class restaurants and hotels in major cities. Fortunately, there have been some recent efforts to shift the harvesting of these orchids from wild-collected to cultivated crops. For example, a number of small-scale terrestrial orchid gardens have been established in several regions. Over time, it is hoped that these gardens will be significantly expanded, and thus help to satisfy the increasing demand for *chikanda* with sustainably grown tubers.[30]

Faham Tea

For centuries, the local populations living on the islands of Réunion and Mauritius have used the fragrant leaves of the orchid plant *Jumellea fragrans* (syn. *Angraccum fragrans*) for flavouring. Locally it was known as *faham* (or *fa'am*). Some have described the scent as being vanilla-like and it was frequently used to make a tea by steeping the dried leaves of the plant. However, in the mid-1800s, a French firm saw a commercial opportunity and began marketing this orchid leaf tea in Paris under the name of Faham. It did have some moderate success, being marketed as an alternative (and caffeine-free) version of normal tea. The (translated) inscription on the packages that were widely available in Paris read:

> It possesses a taste differing greatly from that of tea, and is preferred by the majority of persons who have tasted it. It can be used as a substitute for tea on all occasions, as it combines its tonic and digestive qualities, free from the sleepless effect. It possesses an aroma of great delicacy, capable of being rendered more or less pungent according to the quantity used, and it gives forth a most agreeable perfume; after being drunk it leaves a lasting fragrance in the mouth, and in a closed room the odour of it can be recognised long after.[31]

Faham also became a moderately popular flavouring: a prominent guide to making sweet treats from 1905 suggested that it could be 'used to flavor custards and ices' and that it 'may be of interest to confectioners who are on the alert for novelties'.[32] However, after several decades the distributor found the venture to be no longer profitable and Faham tea and flavourings ceased to be available outside the islands of Réunion and Mauritius.

Flowers and Leaves

In tropical regions, where few terrestrial orchids grow, people have primarily consumed the tender young leaves or young pseudobulbs of epiphytic orchids. The young leaves of *Ceratostylis latifolia* and *Phalaenopsis amabilis* were eaten, both raw and cooked, in western Java; the leaves of *Epiblastus cuneatus* and *Goodyera rubicunda* were eaten in New Guinea; while in Korea the young leaves of *Liparis japonica* were lightly boiled and consumed as a vegetable.[33] The leaves of the crucifix orchid (*Epidendrum ibaguense*) are also consumed (some say they taste similar to either watermelon or cucumber). Also, the starchy stems of *D. speciosum* are sometimes roasted and eaten.[34]

Orchid flower salad, including cultivated *Dendrobium* flowers.

The flowers of various *Dendrobium* and *Epidendrum* species are commonly used in cooking. In some Asian recipes, *Dendrobium* flowers are incorporated into stir-fries, either plain or deep-fried with batter.[35] Orchid flowers are also used in salads, or as a garnish for entrées and desserts such as cakes Recently, a number of niche food markets in North America have begun to offer pre-packaged, edible orchid flowers. These tend to have sweet-tasting petals, while the white bases of the flowers can have a slightly bitter flavour.

Vanilla

Vanilla is by far the most widely cultivated and widely consumed orchid. It is also the only orchid variety that produces a substantial and fleshy fruit – long thin berries that we normally (but incorrectly) refer to as vanilla beans. It is these fruits, not the orchid's flowers, that give us vanilla flavouring and fragrance. However, the fruits need to ripen and cure over a span of many months before they exhibit their familiar vanilla flavour and aroma. In total, there are currently 118 recognized species in the *Vanilla* genus. Twenty-two species are found in Africa; 28 are found in Asia; fourteen are located in North America (including Mexico and the Caribbean); and 54 can be found in Central and South America.[36] There are just three species of *Vanilla* that are commercially cultivated: *Vanilla tahitensis*, *Vanilla pompona* and *Vanilla planifolia*. By far, *Vanilla planifolia* is the most prevalent and commonly consumed variety.

Compared to other species of orchid, not only does *Vanilla planifolia* produce a unique fruit, it is special in the way that it grows and develops. The plant first emerges as a terrestrial orchid, but will soon latch onto the trunk of a nearby tree. With its terrestrial roots still embedded in the soil, it will gradually transform into a climbing vine. As it climbs, it will produce aerial roots at various intervals along its stem, helping it to cling to the tree. As a vine, *Vanilla planifolia* is capable of climbing to a height of well over 20 metres (65 ft). Eventually, if left unattended, many of these plants will break away from their terrestrial

Flowers of the *Vanilla planifolia* orchid range across colours of white, green and yellow.

root anchors, and transform into fully epiphytic plants. Upon becoming an epiphyte, the stems and leaves of the plant will become increasingly succulent.

The flowers of *Vanilla planifolia* are very short-lived and remain open only for a few hours. However, in the right conditions, the vine will flower profusely and continuously for several weeks. Unlike almost every other variety of orchid, the flowers do not produce clumps of pollinia, but instead create individual grains of pollen.[37] In its native Mexico, *V. planifolia* is most commonly pollinated by native bees (most likely *Eulaema meriana* or *Euglossa* sp.), and occasionally by other insects. After pollination, *V. planifolia* will produce long slender fruits (sometimes as long as 30 centimetres/12 in.). The fruit's numerous small seeds are also unique in the orchid family: rather than being 'papery' thin without any stores of nutrition (endosperm), they develop into hard black spheres which do actually contain very small amounts of stockpiled nutrition.[38]

Origins of Vanilla

V. planifolia has its origins in what is now southeast Mexico, in the state of Veracruz. Various Mesoamerican cultural groups would use wild-collected vanilla beans as a flavouring in their food and drinks, perhaps beginning as early as 3,000 years ago. The Olmecs (*c.* 1150–400 BCE) invented a drink that consisted of ground corn and chilli and was flavoured with vanilla. The Toltec peoples and the Mayans also used vanilla flavouring in their food and drink.

It is believed that some of these groups may have engaged in some limited cultivation of *Vanilla* species, perhaps planting vine cuttings in their community gardens. However, it is the Totonac people who have been credited with the most organized and wide-scale cultivation of the genus. The Totonac civilization emerged in the southern part of what is now Mexico. By around the 1200s they had established the Totonac capital city of Papantla. By this time, vanilla had become an integral part not only of their cuisine but of their culture and religion. The Totonacs would frequently scent their temples with a mixture of vanilla and copal tree resin.[39] They believed that the plant had supernatural origins, and a popular legend emerged in their oral storytelling traditions.

Although there are many different interpretations of the Totonac legend, one has been carefully compiled and interpreted from the oral traditions by Professor J. Núñez Domínguez. Recently, Juan Hernández-Hernández has translated this version into English:

> At the summit of a mountain close to Papantla was the temple of Tonacayohua, the goddess of food and planting crops. During the reign of King Teniztli III, one of his wives gave birth to a daughter whose beauty was so great that she was named Tzacopontziza ('Bright Star at Sunrise'), and was consecrated to the cult of Tonacayohua.
>
> As time passed, a young prince named Zkatán Oxga ('Young Deer') and Tzacopontziza fell in love, knowing that this sacrilege was condemned by death.

Vanilla on the vine, from the Florentine Codex, 1580s.

One day, Bright Star at Sunrise left the temple to look for tortillas to offer to Tonacayohua, and fled with the young prince to the jagged mountains in the distance. Not before long [*sic*], a monster appeared and surrounded them by a wall of flames, and ordered them to return.

When the couple returned to the temple, a group of irate priests had been waiting for them, and before ZkatánOxga could say anything, the young lovers were shot with darts, and their bodies were brought to a temple where their hearts were removed, and their carcasses were thrown down into a canyon.

In the place where the bodies landed there was a herb, and its leaves started to wilt as if the scattered blood of the victims had scorched the plant like a curse. Sometime later a new tree began to grow, and within days its vigorous growth covered all the ground around it with its brilliant foliage.

When finally it stopped growing, next to its trunk began to grow an orchid that climbed and also was amazingly vigorous. Within a short amount of time, it had branched and covered the trunk of the tree with its fragile and elegant leaves, and protected by the tree, the orchid grew more until it took the form of a woman lying in the embrace of her lover.

One day the orchid became covered with small flowers and the whole area was filled with an exquisite aroma. Attracted to the pleasant smell, the priests and the pueblo came to observe, and no one doubted that the blood of the young lovers had transformed into the tree and the climbing orchid.

To their surprise, the beautiful little flowers also transformed into large, thin fruits. When the fruits matured, they released a sweet, subtle perfume whose essence invoked the innocent soul of Bright Star at Sunrise and the most exotic fragrances.[40]

As agricultural production of *Vanilla* continued to increase, Totonac farmers began to trade in it with neighbouring peoples and civilizations.

Things changed dramatically for the Totonacs when the Aztecs arrived. Ceasing their nomadic lifestyle, the Aztecs founded their capital city (at the site on which Mexico City now stands) in about 1325, and then began systematically to conquer surrounding civilizations. When they conquered the *Vanilla*-farming Totonacs, they forced them to remit large quantities of the cured fruits as duty. The Aztecs soon developed a great desire for vanilla, and began adding it into their own popular and invigorating chocolate drink which they called *xocolatl*. This beverage contained ground cacao seeds, ground corn, chilli peppers and copious amounts of vanilla. The Aztecs began to consume great quantities of the stuff. In fact, Montezuma II, who ruled over the Aztec Empire from 1502 to 1520, is said to have drunk as many as fifty cups per day.

The renowned Mexican painter Diego Rivera commemorated the two civilizations, the Aztecs and the Totonacs (and their reverence for vanilla), in one of his public murals at the Palacio Nacional in Mexico City. The mural depicts an exchange between the leader of the Totonacs and the leader of the Aztecs, in which the Totonac chief presents his tributes to the Aztec chief. Between the two leaders stands a tall vanilla vine, which is in flower. The Totonac peoples continue to grow vanilla orchids to this day, and the city of Papantla still celebrates its annual Vanilla Festival.

Upon the Spanish Conquest of Mexico in 1521, the Aztec leaders offered Cortés and his fellow conquistadors their *xocolatl*. Although the Spanish did not appear to appreciate the bitter drink, they were quick to recognize the potential of vanilla. Soon, the Spanish began shipping quantities of cured vanilla beans to Europe. Initially these were blended with chocolate, which served to soften its bitterness, and this was enjoyed by wealthy Spaniards.

Vanilla was subsequently exported to the rest of Europe. In England, it was particularly enjoyed by Queen Elizabeth I (r. 1558–1603), who

Detail of a painted mural by Diego Rivera, located on the courtyard walls
of the Palacio Nacional in Mexico City. The mural depicts the meeting of the leader
of the Totonac nation (left) and the leader of the Aztec nation (right). The Totanacs
were compelled to give large quantities of their cultivated vanilla orchids to the
conquering Aztecs. A vanilla vine is depicted growing up from between the feet
of the two leaders, and its flowers are visible near the head of the Aztec leader.

entered a phase, it is said, where she would only drink and eat food
that was flavoured with vanilla.⁴¹ French chefs also discovered vanilla
and began incorporating it into many of their foods, desserts and ice
cream. It also became a common flavouring ingredient in tobacco and
was incorporated into perfumes.

Thomas Jefferson, the third U.S. president (1801–9), is credited
with introducing vanilla-flavoured ice cream to Americans. Jefferson
had previously served as minister to France from 1785 to 1789, and
while in Paris he enjoyed eating French vanilla ice cream. When he
returned to America he brought with him the recipe and a substantial
supply of vanilla beans. As president, he would often serve the un-
common ice cream to his guests. The next president, James Madison

Vanilla beans drying in the sun.

(1809–17), and his wife Dolley continued this vanilla ice-cream tradition, regularly serving it at dinner parties and state functions.[42]

Growing Vanilla

The Totonac people in Veracruz, Mexico, continued to produce vanilla, and were the major global source of vanilla orchids until the mid-1800s. However, their production of Mexican vanilla remained on a limited scale and prices were exorbitant. It was only when the French set up extensive productions of their own on Réunion, and eventually in Madagascar (which would later come under French control), that the marketplace changed significantly.

Initially, the French attempts at vanilla farming were unsuccessful. Unlike Mexico, Réunion lacked the plant's natural pollinators; so, although the orchids would flower, they would not produce fruit. Experiments in hand pollination were attempted, but the success rate was very low. Then, in 1841, Edmond Albius, a twelve-year-old boy who was enslaved on a Réunion vanilla plantation, perfected a simple and reliable method of hand pollination. Almost immediately,

Edmond Albius, illustrated here as a man in his thirties, perfected
a hand-pollination method of the *Vanilla planifolia* when he was just twelve years old.
This method effectively revolutionized the international vanilla industry.

this had a profound impact on the global vanilla industry. Much more plentiful and reliable supplies of vanilla could now be attained.

Vanilla plants are normally propagated from cuttings which are then planted in soil at the bases of trees. While juveniles, *Vanilla* plants depend heavily on soil-based mycorrhizal fungi for healthy development. However, as the plants mature, they rely less on soil nutrients (and soil-based mycorrhizal fungi) and can become entirely epiphytic (where they will engage with, but to a lesser degree, a different species of mycorrhizal fungi).[43] In order to ensure that the cultivated vanilla vine remains primarily a terrestrial orchid (and therefore is ensured robust engagement with its soil-based mycorrhizal fungi), a very specific method has been developed. As the cultivated vanilla vine grows up a tree, it is looped back down after reaching a height of about 2 metres (6½ ft). The vine is trained all the way back down to the ground and then it is encouraged back upwards again. At the base of this loop, the vine is submerged into the soil, where it will then form more terrestrial roots that will burrow into the ground. This process will be repeated after the upward-growing vine loop has again reached a height of 2 metres. This ensures that the very long vine (which would normally climb to a height of 20 metres (65 ft) or more) remains at a height where workers can easily pollinate the flowers and harvest the beans.[44] Importantly, this also ensures that the vine remains a terrestrial plant and thus has access to more mycorrhizal fungi, ensuring that the plant maintains vigorous growth throughout its lifespan.

It takes about three years after planting the vanilla vines before they will begin flowering freely.[45] In order to achieve a viable crop, the flowers require hand pollination. (This is now also the case in Mexico, as native pollinating insects appear to be less abundant and less effective than they were in the past.) Although the vanilla vines are receptive to manual self-fertilization, the flowers contain structures that prevent this from occurring naturally. The main impediment is that the flowers contain what is called a 'rostellum' which 'hangs exactly in between the stigma (female organ) and the anther sac (male organ)'. This rostellum prevents the flower's own pollen from coming into contact with its own stigma.[46] Juan Hernández-Hernández has outlined the steps that are involved in order to bypass the rostellum and successfully force the flower to self-pollinate:

1. Use a toothpick or similar tool to make a longitudinal slit in the labellum on the side opposite of the column to reveal the reproductive structures.
2. With the same end of the toothpick, lift underneath the rostellum and flip vertically so that the anther sac can hang down unimpeded over the stigma lobes.
3. Gently press the anther to the stigma until the two stick together and then remove the toothpick.[47]

Vanilla flowers are very short-lived. They generally open very early in the morning (just before sunrise) and are closed and withering by 12 noon. This leaves, generally, a five- to seven-hour window in which the flowers are most receptive to pollination. Needless to say, this process requires a very delicate touch, but an experienced worker can pollinate up to a thousand flowers in a five-hour period.[48] Vanilla flowers do not open all at once, so human pollinators are required to inspect each vine daily to see if any flowers have opened, throughout the entire two-month period that the vines may be in flower. However, only about two-thirds of the vine's flowers are hand-pollinated, allowing the plants to have enough energy to produce larger, higher-quality fruit.

Unlike most other orchids, the vanilla fruit will begin to develop almost immediately after pollination. Within about 45 days, they will have reached their full size of 15 to 25 centimetres (6 to 10 in.) in length; but these will be left to slowly mature on the vine over the next seven to eight months.[49] Fruits are harvested when they begin to yellow at the tip, which occurs some nine to ten months after pollination. However, because each fruit on a vine may have been pollinated on a different day – sometimes weeks apart – they will not be ready for harvest at the same time. So, as with pollination, harvesting becomes a meticulous daily task, spanning a two-month period.

When harvested, the fruits still lack the characteristic vanilla flavour or fragrance; this will be expressed through a lengthy curing process. If the fruits were to be left on the vine, they would eventually begin to exhibit some noticeable vanilla aroma, but the beans would also become withered, curled and much less potent than the result that can be achieved through an off-vine curing process. The modern curing process is essentially a variation of the original method that was developed by the Totonac people many centuries ago. It generally takes from three to five months, and it involves painstaking and repetitive sequences of oven drying, sun curing and 'sweating' of the fruit.

Vanilla planifolia growing up a tree trunk. This species can reach up to 30 metres (98 ft).

Vanilla orchid fruit,
or 'beans', at various
stages of ripeness.
The middle bean
is considered ideal
for harvesting,
as its tip is just
beginning to yellow;
the other examples
are considered
either too ripe
or not yet ripe.

In 1847, American chemist Joseph Burnett perfected a method for making vanilla extract. In this way, the vanilla essence could be isolated from the beans and put into a concentrated liquid form. Vanilla extract was very convenient: it was easy to use, easy to ship and had a long shelf life. It was also less expensive, for vanilla extract could be made with inferior-quality beans. To produce extract, the beans are normally cut into small pieces and steeped in alcohol for several months.

Vanilla Substitutes

In 1858, the French scientist Nicola-Théodore Gobley was able to isolate vanilla's main flavour component, vanillin, from the newly available vanilla extracts. A further breakthrough occurred in 1874, when two German chemists, Ferdinand Tiemann and Wilhelm Haarmann, discovered how to synthesize vanillin from the bark of pine trees. Later, other scientists successfully synthesized vanillin from a whole range of raw materials, including clove oil, guaiacol and even coal tar (a thick, black liquid, which is a by-product from the distillation of coal). Vanillin, it turns out, is a fairly simple chemical compound made up of carbon, hydrogen and oxygen ($CH_3OC_6H_3(OH)CHO$) and regardless of its source material, it is considered safe to consume. Although vanillin constitutes the vanilla fruit's main flavour compound, it represents only a portion of the vanilla flavour experience (which consists of hundreds of elements).

As the use of vanillin (and other vanilla substitutes) increased, it began to impact the traditional vanilla industry, and a number of companies (especially the Joseph Burnett Company in America, whose founder was the inventor of vanilla extract) fought to enact industry standards. In his publication from 1900, Burnett claimed 'There is no article sold in America more capable of abuse, more subject to fraud and ignorance, than Vanilla extract.'[50] Soon, however, virtually everything began to be flavoured with either easy-to-use (but moderately expensive) vanilla extract, or easy-to-use (and very cheap) imitation vanilla. Major American food corporations would flavour many of their products (particularly desserts and beverages) with vanilla; for example, the makers of Coca-Cola included vanilla flavouring in nearly all of their mass-produced soft drinks and confectionary.

In fact, by the 1950s, vanilla flavouring was so common that it became something to parody, and vanilla became synonymous with the boring and the mundane. This was highlighted in a 1952 episode of the U.S. radio and television series *The Halls of Ivy*. This series starred the British film acting couple Ronald Colman and Benita (Hume)

Colman, who played the husband-and-wife characters Dr and Mrs Hall. Each episode would feature a sequence in which Dr Hall would pontificate about particular aspects of American culture that exasperated him. One thing that particularly got under his skin was their housekeeper Louisa's reliance on vanilla flavouring.

> MRS HALL: Louisa is cooking you a surprise dessert for dinner.
> DR. HALL: Oh? Something with a pronounced flavour of vanilla?
> MRS HALL: I think so . . . how did you guess?
> DR. HALL: Oh, that was no guess. ALL her desserts are flavoured with vanilla. I think I shall send her an anonymous letter containing the facts of life about chocolate, maple, and cherry!

At this point, the live studio audience roared with laughter, as they clearly understood how thoroughly vanilla had usurped virtually all other flavours in American cuisine. Chocolate or cherry were now considered to be exotic (and provocatively associated with 'the facts of life'), when compared to the modest conventionality of vanilla.

Vanilla-like analogues can also be found in several other forms throughout the natural world. One of the most surprising sources is the North American beaver (*Castor canadensis*) and the Eurasian beaver (*Castor fiber*). These animals have been hunted for thousands of years, not only for their fur and meat but for their scent. Both male *and* female beavers have castor sacs (large testicle-like scent glands) at the posterior end of their bodies which produce castoreum, 'a yellowish, butter-like' substance with a strong aroma. By blending castoreum with their urine stream, the beaver will use this secretion to mark their territories and also to help waterproof their fur. The castor sacs are quite large, up to 8 centimetres (3 in.) wide and 15 centimetres (6 in.) long, and are removed at the same time as the beaver's pelt.[51] (It is, however, also technically possible to 'milk' the beaver of its castoreum while it is anaesthetized.[52])

Humans have been using castoreum as a perfume and incense for hundreds, if not thousands, of years. In its concentrated state, it has an 'animal-sweet' and 'birch, tar-like, musky odor'; however, when diluted with alcohol (as castoreum extract) it takes on a surprisingly pleasant, vanilla-like flavour and aroma. As a result, castoreum has been used in the perfume industry, as well as to scent creams and lotions. It has also been used, very occasionally, as a vanilla flavour substitute in foods, such as ice cream, baked goods, beverages and confectionary.[53] Several years ago, a spate of humorous and sensationalist news articles described the source of castoreum and warned readers that 'beaver butt goo' may be used to flavour their 'vanilla' ice cream![54] Although castoreum is a U.S. Department of Agriculture-approved food ingredient, it is very rarely used today and highly unlikely to be found in any normally sourced food products. It does, however, continue to be used in some sectors of the perfume industry.

Vanilla beans displayed alongside vanilla-flavoured macarons.

Watkins Imitation Vanilla Essence, promoted as 'the flavour that duplicates vanilla', *c.* 1960.

Another source of 'vanilla' substitute can be found in the Brazilian tonka bean, which is harvested from the South American tree *Dipteryx odorata*. The beans contain a compound known as coumarin, and in the early 1900s most artificial vanilla extracts would contain some amount of the substance. Unfortunately, coumarin has been found to be very toxic to humans if ingested in large quantities, and its use as a food additive is now banned in most regions. It does, however, continue to be used as an ingredient in perfumes and cosmetics.

Vanilla Fragrance

Vanilla is one of the most pervasive fragrances, and its aroma is included in a wide range of perfumes, air fresheners and scented candles. It is also added to household cleaning products (even if it is not advertised on the label) in order to make them more appealing. Vanilla may be added to pet foods, in order to make them smell more pleasant to, not the pet, but the human who has purchased the product. It is frequently added to pharmaceutical products such as cough medicine. Surprisingly it is also added to many industrial products, such as bookbinding adhesives and rubber and plastic products (particularly children's plastic toys) in order to mask some of the disagreeable chemical odours found in those materials.[55]

It is estimated that more than 50 per cent of all perfumes contain vanilla.[56] Fine perfumes are often engineered to contain three distinctive notes (or layers) of scent, each becoming prominent at different times as it is being worn. As Luca Turin writes:

> A perfume, once it has become familiar, works like an accurate clock. The procession of odorants, precipitous at first, stately later, tells us where we are in the story. Spray it on after work. The top notes, the first ones to fly out, say it is still early in the evening that feels full of promise. Next come the heart notes, where the perfumer's art really shows itself, where fragrance tries (like us) to be as distinctive, beautiful and intelligent as possible. Lastly by three a.m. the perfume has literally boiled down to its darkest, heaviest molecules at a time when our basest instincts, whether for sleep or other hobbies, manifest themselves.[57]

The majority of popular perfumes incorporate vanilla as part of their base note as it has the unique ability to not only effectively bridge between fragrances, but to persist longer than most.[58] There are also a number of perfumes that feature vanilla more prominently (as either their 'top' or 'heart' notes) and some will even incorporate imagery of the plant into the marketing of the perfume. Some fragrances that distinctively feature vanilla are Shalimar (Guerlain, 1925); Canoe (Dana, 1935); Brut (Fabergé, 1964); Opium (St Laurent, 1977); Obsession (Calvin Klein, 1985); Coco Mademoiselle (Chanel, 2001); and Midnight Fantasy (Britney Spears, 2007).

Recent research has demonstrated that vanilla is a fragrance that exhibits extraordinary olfactory properties. Pure vanilla is aromatically complex, containing at least five hundred different compounds (vanillin being the most prominent), and this complexity contributes greatly to its appeal. Additionally, vanilla is a scent that the human nose is able to detect in incredibly small amounts. We also seem to almost universally like the fragrance, and, contrasting with nearly every other scent, we still like it even if we are inundated with it at very high levels.[59]

Orchid Flower Fragrances

Although vanilla is the most common orchid-themed scent that is used in the production of perfume, various species of orchid flowers have also served as inspiration for fragrances. Curiously, for some time (particularly in North America), orchid flowers had the reputation of having no scent. This was due to the fact that the most common orchids used to make cut flowers and corsages were in fact mostly odourless. However, in Asia, the idea of the orchid flower's beauty and its robust fragrance were seamlessly bound together. Particularly in China, the fragrances of *Cymbidiums* and other orchids were regarded as the 'Number One Fragrance under Heaven', and the Chinese philosopher Confucius (551–479 BCE) is claimed to have mused that 'the orchid grows in the remote forest, where it provides a pleasant fragrance regardless of the scarcity of admirers.'[60]

In fact, about 75 per cent of orchid species do have detectible (at least to human noses) fragrance. Most give off lovely aromas; many have fragrant floral scents, while some smell of cinnamon, coconut, citrus – and some even of chocolate. Flowers of *Cattleya*, *Oncidium* and

Stanhopea fragrance, from the Orchid Flowers Perfume series produced by Seely of Detroit, Michigan, 1890. Other varieties included *Anguloa, Galeandra, Miltonia, Vanda* and *Calanthe* fragrances.

Dendrobium, in particular, feature some of the more aromatic and popular fragrances. It is these that many (non-vanilla) orchid-themed perfumes have either been made from or at least 'inspired' by.

In America during the late 1800s the Seely Manufacturing Company of Detroit, Michigan, began selling a line of perfumes under the registered name Orchid Flowers Perfume. Initially, there were six different scents available: *Anguloa, Calanthe, Galeandra, Miltonia, Stanhopea* and *Vanda* fragrances. At the time, a 2-ounce (60 ml) bottle cost $1.50. These were touted as 'The most exquisite perfumes in existence'. By 1910 there were dozens of different perfume man-ufacturers in North America making a great number of different orchid-themed perfumes. These included George Lorenz Co., with

Butterfly Orchid; Paul Rieger & Co., with California Purple Orchid; Lazell, Dalley & Co., with Orchid Empire; and Mellier Co., with Orchid Bloom. Although some of these early perfumes would have been attained through the distillation of the flower's fragrance, nearly all perfumes today are synthetically created, being simply 'inspired by the exotic scents of orchids'.[61]

Medicinal Orchids

Orchids have been used extensively in traditional medicine for thousands of years, and probably involving thousands of different orchid species. As previously mentioned, in Europe and West Asia, salep (made from terrestrial orchid tubers) was initially used for its purported aphrodisiac properties. It was also claimed to have numerous health and healing benefits. Despite all of these claims being unfounded, its medicinal use does persist in some parts of the world. For example, throat lozenges available in Greece and Turkey will sometimes contain salep.

Odontoglossum crispum, var. *Fastuosum*, from *Lindenia* (1887), vol. III.

Perhaps the biggest consumers of medicinal orchids are those that are involved in Traditional Chinese Medicine (or TCM). One of the most important orchid species in TCM is *Gastrodia elata*, which was originally referred to as Chijian (red arrow) because of its upright red inflorescence. It became known as *Tianma* during the Song dynasty (960–1279 CE). The dried tubers of this species have been used for many medicinal purposes over the centuries, and they are commonly found for sale in Chinese medicine shops and at markets throughout China and other parts of Asia.[62] The dried pseudobulbs of several *Dendrobium* species have also been very important to TCM. The Chinese name for *Dendrobium* is *shihu* (*shi* referring to 'rock' and *hu* referring to 'living'). During the Han dynasty (206 BCE–220 CE), just two species were recognized as medicinal *shihu*: *Dendrobium officinale* and *D. moniliforme*. Both of these could be found growing on rocky terrain in many parts of central China. As the centuries wore on, other *Dendrobium* species from other parts of the country also came to be recognized as medicinal *shihu*, such as *Dendrobium nobile*.[63] Another important orchid in TCM is the hyacinth orchid *Bletilla striata*. In Chinese, it is referred to as *baiji*. In Japan, it is called *Shiran* (purple orchid), while in Vietnam it is referred to as either *Bach cap* or *Hua lan tía*. As with many other species, it is the tuberous roots that are consumed.[64]

Hundreds of other species of orchids have been used in both TCM and in Ayurvedic (traditional Hindu) medicine. Despite their traditional medicinal roles over the span of many centuries, their use is supported by exceedingly few modern scientific or clinical studies. But due to their long historical use and also due to the fact that many orchid plants contain a range of novel alkaloids, some believe that eventually they *might* provide provable health benefits.[65] Interestingly, the hyacinth orchid *Bletilla striata* has been used recently in clinical studies, and may show some promise in the treatment of inflammation and liver problems.[66] Unfortunately, as a majority of these orchids come from wild-collected sources, their continued use critically impacts orchid populations.

Recently there has been a great deal of research into human tissue engineering: that is, seeking to grow human tissue in a lab, which can be used to repair injured skin or muscle. Thus far, scientists have found it is fairly easy to grow human tissue in layers or as amorphous blobs, but growing it in more defined three-dimensional formations for specialized skin, bone or muscle regrowth requires existing structures or scaffolds for it to grow upon. It turns out that plants have an ideal 'vasculature system' to enable such tissue engineering. One of the plants that have been successfully used in the trialling of human cell adhesion to plant tissue is the orchid *Laelia anceps*.[67]

Disa bracteata (South African weed orchid) has become
a highly invasive weed in some parts of Australia.

seven

Orchid Conservation

ʒഗ

Despite the general pervasiveness of orchids, many species are severely threatened in the wild. In large measure, this is a result of sustained human activity.

The earliest wholesale destruction of wild terrestrial orchids originated during the salep craze, which began in the Ottoman Empire and spread throughout Europe and England. Although humans had been regularly consuming orchid tubers for nourishment for many thousands of years, this was the first time that they were harvested en masse – and almost entirely due to a pointless dietary fad based on erroneous health claims. Unfortunately, wide-scale and unsustainable salep consumption has persisted. Similarly, *chikanda* (the African dish derived from orchid tubers) is becoming an increasingly sought-after cuisine. The continued medicinal use of wild-collected orchid tubers in TCM is also putting vast pressure on terrestrial orchid populations.

The era known as 'orchidmania' is what really started the wholesale decimation of tropical epiphytic orchid populations. At its peak, in the mid- to late 1800s, millions of orchid plants were ripped from their natural habitats each year, and shipped off to England, Europe and the United States. Not only were the orchids removed from habitat, but much of their environment was severely damaged. There were very few who expressed concern aimed at stopping this plundering at the time, but writing in 1895, Benjamin Samuel Williams warned:

There is another great evil attending importations, but this occurs in their native country; the plants are heedlessly torn from their natural habitats, which are sometimes ruthlessly cleared of the beautiful flowers that cannot be replaced in the locality. We are sorry to hear of some of our collectors having so little respect for these treasures of nature's production that they gather all they can, having no regard for the future, and not even leaving a few plants in the locality to increase and multiply by shedding their seed to germinate naturally over the mountains, rocks, and trees. If this kind of work continues, there will be but few Orchids left, excepting where the collectors cannot get at them.[1]

Williams concluded by noting, what would seem very obvious to us today, 'It is to be feared that some of our collectors do not go for the love of the plants, but to make all they can for the time being.'[2]

Rock orchid (*Dendrobium speciosum*), an Australian lithophytic/epiphytic orchid.

Aganisia cyanea, from
Lindenia (1887), vol. III.

Some fifty years later, Australian author J. Murray Cox published
A Cultural Table of Orchidaceous Plants. He concludes this hefty volume with
an original 147-line poem titled 'The Complaint of a Cattleya', in
which he describes the suffering of a wild-collected epiphyte, but told
from the orchid's point of view. The opening stanza reads:

> Torn incontinently from my harbourage
> High on a tree which through the centuries
> Has raised a noble head 'midst its primeval brethren –
> Thrown, numbed and bruised, in a fuggy box –
> Thence in a dark and noisome hold,
> Transported o'er the uncertain waves
> Until I came at last to rest, fatigued, half-starved
>   and 'all-alone',
> 'Midst some four hundred and four score

Sad exiled plants – who stood in serried ranks
On benches in a heated house;
Or hung, like felons, from a beam
Athwart the glass roof.[3]

To add emphasis to his poem, the author recalls how, when he was a young boy, orchids were ubiquitous throughout Australian bushlands and forests. From his vantage point of 1946, he laments how few of these remain; from our vantage of the present day, the situation seems increasingly dire.

The urge to over-collect desirable orchid species has been a significant problem throughout the world. Originally, orchid nurseries would deal exclusively in wild-collected plants, both native and imported. Although orchids could fetch enormous prices, many species that were deemed common would go for exceptionally low prices. For example, at the turn of the century, one could purchase lots of a thousand native North American orchid plants for as little as $5. Such vast wholesale numbers would certainly have helped to make these common orchids much less common. In England, the lady's slipper orchid (*Cypripedium calceolus*) was so depleted from its habitat that by 1920 there was reported to be just one single plant remaining in the wild, within the whole of the British Isles.[4] Fortunately, by the late 1920s, reliable strategies for seed propagation had been developed and this, very gradually, began to reduce the pressure on wild populations of both epiphytes and terrestrials. This reprieve has been further assisted in recent decades by the introduction of tissue culture propagation.

A significant amount of illegal orchid trading continues to this day, despite the fact that there are a range of international and local laws that seek to control the collection and trade of virtually all orchid species. One mechanism to help stem the tide of illegal trade has come about through the creation of the Convention on International Trade in Endangered Species of Wild Flora and Fauna (CITES), a major international treaty that aims to protect endangered flora and fauna, including threatened and endangered orchids. The treaty maintains a list of all internationally protected specimens, divided into different categories. Species that are listed in appendix I are heavily protected and described as being at serious risk from commercial trade. The orchids include *Cattleya trianaei*, *Dendrobium cruentum*, *Laelia lobata*, *Peristeria elata* (dove orchid) and all of the species of *Paphiopedilum*; international trade in these field-collected specimens is essentially banned. Most species of orchids are listed in appendix II; international trade in these field-collected specimens is very strictly regulated. Because orchid species are so numerous (and threatened) they make up a staggering 70 per cent of all plants listed in CITES appendices I and II.[5] Enforcement of these laws and regulations has proved difficult, but there are a number of innovations that have the potential to make greater enforcement possible. For example, it has previously been impossible to ascertain what species have been used once the orchid tubers have been ground up and made into salep or *chikanda*. However, new DNA-based techniques can now identify precisely which species were used as ingredients.[6]

The spread of online trade in illegal plants has also increased dramatically in recent years, and rare or newly discovered species can still attract vast sums. Online sales have brought illegal plants within easier reach of the average consumer, and in many cases the buyer may not even realize that the plants they are purchasing were illegally collected.[7]

Orchid Habitats

In more recent decades, it is undeniably the loss of habitat that has posed the greatest threat to orchids. Land clearing and logging have destroyed much of the world's tropical forests, thus destroying much of the world's epiphytic orchid habitats. For example, a major orchid-rich forest in Brazil, the Mata Atlantica, now covers less than 4 per cent of its original range.[8] Terrestrial orchids are also threatened by expanding human development into both wilderness and rural areas.

Land clearing and development also destroy the physical structures that orchids grow upon: epiphytes need tall established trees; lithophytes need large rocks and cliff faces. Habitat loss destroys not only the orchids but their pollinators, their fungi and other important associated life forms.

However, it isn't just the Amazon jungles, the forests of Borneo and other pristine wilderness areas where orchid habitats have been

Orchids print illustrated by C. Philipp, depicting a range of orchid species, from a German text published by Bibliographisches Institut Leipzig, 1895.

lost. In urban areas such as Singapore, wild orchids had managed to survive alongside humans for centuries. However, in recent years these populations have suffered great losses; 'Over the past 51 years of rapid urbanization, Singapore has had 178 of 226 native orchid species extinct and 40 critically endangered, due to extensive habitat loss.'[9]

Many orchid species, even before they had to contend with human-led destruction of habitats and over-collecting, would naturally produce very limited population numbers. This represents an intriguing paradox with orchids: they are extremely widespread, yet many species are effectively niche plants and maintain very limited populations. For example:

> *Phragmipedium exstaminodium* and *Mexipedium xerophyticum* from Mexico are known from 30 and 11 wild plants respectively; the Australian *Calochilus richiae* is known from fewer than 20 plants in its native Victoria; and only three populations of *Paphiopedilum rothschildianum* are known on Mt Kinabalu.[10]

So, the destruction of habitat of just a few hectares can cause multiple species to become functionally extinct.

A healthy distribution of appropriate species of mycorrhizal fungi is essential to the success of wild orchids. Much still needs to be learned about these partnerships – and although a great many matching fungi are being identified and isolated, these fungi can also have very specific habitat requirements. For example, some orchids grow in soils that would be considered toxic to other plants, but where their companion fungi are able to thrive.[11] Another layer of complexity is that orchids will often rely on more than one type of fungus, as many orchids will switch fungi as the plants mature. So, scientists are finding that it is sometimes useful to isolate fungal partners from seedlings (or protocorms) as well as from mature plant specimens.[12]

The two main approaches to orchid conservation are referred to as *in situ*, the protection of plants in their native habitat (arguably the most effective); and *ex situ*, the cultivation of orchids away from their habitat, in botanic gardens or private collections. A number of conservationists have cautioned that relying purely on the latter method will have a negative long-term effect on the genetic variability of the plants. Unquestionably, given the fact that orchids have such complex ecological requirements, it is best for orchids to be conserved in their natural habitat – that is, *in situ*. Of course, when there is no other option and to help hedge against inevitable habitat destruction (particularly of species with very small populations) and increasing threats of global warming, *ex situ* conservation techniques do clearly have a role to play. Some significant and very vital conservation work has been achieved by a number of botanical organizations in this area, including the Royal Botanic Gardens at Kew.

It is common practice for scientists and conservationists to collect and store seeds from species that are threatened, in order to help ensure their continued success. Fortunately, most orchid seeds appear to be amenable to long-term storage, by simply drying them and maintaining them at low temperatures; and in some cases, there has also been success in storing orchid protocorms.[13]

Rather ironically, it was once believed that orchids were impossible to hybridize. James Bateman, speaking in 1885, recalled how several years earlier he had paid a visit to a plant collection belonging to his friend Mr Huntly, who held staunchly anti-hybrid views: 'My first orchid-growing friend was Mr. Huntly. When I paid Mr. Huntly a visit at his snug rectory in Huntingdonshire, he pointed out to me his cacti and his Orchids, and said, "I like those plants, in fact they are the only plants I grow, because those fiends (meaning the hybridizers) cannot touch them."'[14]

Of course, Mr Huntly was wrong about both plant families – especially regarding orchids, as there are now well over 100,000 registered hybrids, and undoubtedly countless more unregistered ones. In a similar vein, orchid enthusiast Barney Greer wrote more recently of the genus *Stanhopea*: 'It's tempting, if you have two Stanhopeas in flower at the one time, to be "creative" and make a random hybrid

Pl. 9

L. ÆLIA AUTUMNALIS.

Laelia autumnalis, from James Bateman.
The Orchidaceae of Mexico and Guatemala (1837–43).

for fun. Resist the temptation – you won't invent anything more fantastic than what exists already, but if you "self" a disappearing species you will be doing the world a good turn."[5] As impressive, beautiful and sought after as many orchid hybrids are, most specialists agree that an important strategy of *ex situ* orchid conservation is to ensure that there are adequate numbers of natural orchid species in collections. Accordingly, there are a number of orchid societies that are dedicated especially to the preservation and cultivation of these natural orchid species.

Orchid Weeds

Not all orchids are endangered, niche plants. Surprisingly, there are a number of orchid species that appear to be quite widespread and 'weedy'. For example, some terrestrial orchids will do very well in

Orchid cultivar.

Chysis laevis, from
James Bateman,
*The Orchidaceae of
Mexico and Guatemala*
(1837–43).

CHYSIS LAEVIS.

disturbed soil, alongside where humans have built roads, planted lawns and cleared land. These orchids, many of which are capable of self-fertilizing, will produce a large quantity of wind-dispersed seeds, and many are also able to propagate vegetatively. As an example, Richard Mabey describes his native English bee orchid:

> Bee orchids are equipped with some familiar weed technol-
> ogy. The flowers produce many thousands of dust-like
> seeds, which can be blown great distances on the wind. If
> they come down on disturbed chalk soils they can build up
> huge colonies of flowering stems. Old quarries are the classic
> bee orchid location. More conspicuously they've appeared
> in numbers on the spoil tips of chemical factories, on a new
> roundabout outside Hitchin, at the edge of the car park at

the Milton Keynes Telephone Exchange and on the running track of a smart private school in Oxfordshire.[16]

Mabey also describes how hundreds of these orchids have been known to sprout up and flower within a small patch of grass   posing a dilemma for the gardener, as they ponder whether or not to mow their lawn.

This tendency to grow in disturbed sites became celebrated in Ireland when it was noticed that 'purple orchis . . . bloomed in great profusion on some of the bomb sites of Belfast in 1941.' Because these orchids were able to grow from these sites of destruction (seemingly withstanding a bomb blast) they became associated with good fortune. Subsequently, the flowers also gained the reputation of helping to keep away misfortune and evil, and they would regularly be placed on windowsills for good luck.[17]

Several other terrestrial orchid species have become known for their weedy nature. For example, the broad-leaved helleborine (*Epipactis helleborine*), which is native to Europe and the Middle East, was accidentally introduced into the eastern coast of the United States. Within a matter of decades, it had spread throughout most of North America.[18] Similarly, the tropical terrestrial orchid, soldier's lawn orchid (*Zeuxine strateumatica*), native to Asia, can now be found in such places as Brazil and the southern states of the United States. It has even been reported growing wild in urban areas of Florida.[19] The terrestrial cow's tongue orchid (*Oeceoclades maculata*), which is native to Africa, has now colonized many parts of the Americas. Its succulent leaves seem to be of great advantage as it spreads into areas with inconsistent rainfall. It also does not require insects for pollination, and can self-pollinate; it does so with the assistance of intermittent falling raindrops, which first dislodge the pollinia, and subsequently flush them into contact with the stigma of the column.[20] One or two orchid species have even become so prevalent that they are now regarded as highly invasive weeds; an example is the South African orchid (*Disa bracteata*) that now populates wide areas of Australian grasslands.[21]

As a result of climate change, some orchids that are normally found only in warm Mediterranean climates are now being identified in areas much further north. For example, the small-flowered tongue orchid (*Serapias parviflora*), which is usually found in southern France, Spain and Portugal, has recently been discovered in England.[22] Similarly, the giant orchid (*Himantoglossum robertianum*), which normally grows in Greece, can now be found growing in parts of rural England.[23] Global warming is also having an impact on epiphytic orchids, as increasing temperatures are drying out epiphytes growing in the upper canopies of trees.[24] Lowland species are now being found at much higher altitudes than before. More worrying is that the altered climates are detrimentally affecting pollinator populations and their ability to effectively carry out their pollination duties.[25]

Orchid Societies

Orchid societies play a number of important roles. For one they bring together people who share a love of orchids. People join established orchid societies for a wide range of reasons, but many do so to gain access to plants that cannot be purchased at the local nursery (or supermarket), to learn more about orchids and to meet people who share a similar interest. Members range from highly specialized botanists to hobbyists who simply like having a few orchids as house plants. Societies hold regular meetings that feature guest speakers, discussions, plant sales and exhibits. Larger societies also hold conferences that feature nationally and internationally recognized speakers. Such conferences might incorporate exhibitions, workshops, plant sales and excursions to significant gardens and collections. Each year, societies will hold orchid shows and competitions (normally open to the public), which help foster excellence in the growing and presentation of spectacular orchid specimens. These competitions also serve to educate the public about orchids and to attract new members. Another important role of these societies, particularly in recent decades, has been to facilitate the conservation, cultivation and scientific

Tongue orchid (*Dockrillia linguiformis*, syn. *Dendrobium linguiforme*),
an Australian lithophytic and epiphytic orchid.

study of orchids. Many societies will sponsor field studies, habitat preservation and other conservation efforts.

As a reflection of their ongoing popularity, there are now many hundreds of orchid societies (local, national and international) across the world. One of the first orchid-growing societies was founded in 1897 in Manchester, England. The American Orchid Society was founded in 1921.

Orchid Futures

Orchids are tremendously complex and we still have a long way to go to fully understand the relationships that they forge with their pollinators, with their associated mycorrhizal fungi and with the rest of their natural world. We have discovered some 28,000 species of orchids, and we undoubtedly still have many more to discover. Likewise, there are well over 100,000 orchid hybrids – and we undoubtedly still have many more to create.

From this perspective, orchids are seemingly everywhere – and they seem to be forever expanding their footprint. On the other hand, many wild orchids are severely threatened due to habitat destruction, over-collecting and worsening climate change. If this trajectory continues, it is quite possible that we will see an increase of 'weedy' orchids – of a few resilient terrestrial species – but a vast reduction in rarer small-population epiphytic orchids. We can only hope that our impact on the planet will lessen, habitat destruction will slow and that our understanding of these plants will grow; and most importantly that our empathy will flower along with our orchid friends.

Given our own uncertain times, it might be worthwhile to look back to the year 1892, when Frederick Boyle mused: 'I sometimes think that orchids were designed at their inception to comfort the elect of human beings in this anxious age.'[26] Orchids have had a surprising degree of impact – they have pervaded our art, our culture, our history, our gardens and our cuisine. Their current popularity also shows no sign of abating. Fortunately, this is not the end.

Paphiopedilum cultivar.

Timeline

206 BCE–220 CE	During the Han dynasty, Chinese nobility begin cultivating orchid plants. Earliest known Chinese herbal text, *Shen Nong Bencao Jing*, promotes several different species of orchids for medicinal purposes
9 BCE	The Early Roman *Ara Pacis* (Altar to Peace) is built by Augustus and incorporates a floral frieze depicting orchid flowers
40–90 CE	Orchids are mentioned in *Herball of Dioscorides*, written by Pedanius Dioscorides
c. 1400	During the Ming dynasty, orchids are incorporated into the concept of 'four noble plants' (plum blossom, orchid, chrysanthemum and bamboo) and subsequently become an important part of 'Chinese literati art'
c. 1495	*The Unicorn in Captivity* tapestry (part of the *Unicorn Tapestries*) is created, and depicts an orchid flower
1500s	Salep (beverage made from terrestrial orchid tubers) gains popularity throughout the Ottoman Empire
1583	Carolus Clusius publishes herbal, *Atrebatis rariorum*, in Austria, which includes orchid information and illustrations
1597	John Gerard's *Generall Historie of Plantes*, published in London, includes substantial information on and illustrations of terrestrial orchids

c. 1599	William Shakespeare mentions orchids in *Hamlet*
1637	Tulipmania, the tulip craze that swept Holland, abruptly ends when the speculative tulip market crashes
1700s	Salep (known as saloop) becomes increasingly popular in England
1706	French gardening writer Louis Liger invents a story describing the mythical origins of the orchid, which he sets within the era of ancient Greek mythology
1731	London-based horticulturist Peter Collinson receives a new orchid, *Bletia verecunda* (syn. *Helleborine americana*), from Providence Island in the Bahamas. The plant blooms in the following year, 1732
1787	*Curtis's Botanical Magazine* commences publication under founding editor William Curtis. It contains many articles and illustrations featuring orchids
1793	Christian Konrad Sprengel describes how some orchid flowers, by not providing nectar rewards, are most likely misleading their pollinators
1818	William Cattley receives an unexpected, dried orchid from Brazil, which subsequently produces a stunning flower. The orchid is later named after him, *Cattleya labiata*. Some point to this as the starting date of orchidmania
1824	John Lindley creates a whole new genus of orchids, *Cattleya*, after British horticulturalist William Cattley
1830s	Dr Nathaniel Bagshaw Ward invents the Wardian case
1837	Commencement of Queen Victoria's reign (1837–1901), which more or less coincides with the era of orchidmania
1837–43	James Bateman publishes his large volume *The Orchidaceae of Mexico and Guatemala*
1841	Edmond Albius, a twelve-year-old slave working on a Réunion Vanilla plantation, perfects a simple and reliable method of hand-pollinating Vanilla flowers

1847	American chemist Joseph Burnett perfects a method for making vanilla extract
1852	*The Orchid-Growers Manual* by Benjamin Samuel Williams is published
1853	John Dominy creates one of the first successful orchid hybrids, crossing two species of *Cattleya* (*C. guttata* × *C. loddigesii*)
1858	French scientist Nicola-Théodore Gobley isolates vanillin, the main flavour component of vanilla beans
1862	Charles Darwin's book *The Various Contrivances by Which Orchids Are Fertilised by Insects* is published (revised and expanded 2nd edn, 1877)
1875	Charles Darwin's book *Insectivorous Plants* is published
1877	Alfred Russel Wallace publishes scientific article on the orchid mantis
1879	Australian travel writer James Hingston publishes his popular book *The Australian Abroad*, which erroneously describes a carnivorous flower (which was actually an orchid mantis)
1880	Charles Darwin's *The Power of Movement in Plants* is published
1889	Tiffany & Co. begin producing a series of highly realistic orchid brooches designed by jewellery maker George Paulding Farnham
1890s	Joseph Chamberlain (1836–1914) emerges as a notable British politician and statesman, known for his trademark monocle and orchid flower pinned to his lapel
1891	The first 'skull orchid' is put on display at Protheroe's auction house in London in the lead-up to a major orchid auction
1894	H. G. Wells's short story 'The Flowering of the Strange Orchid' is published
1895	George Hansen publishes his book *The Orchid Hybrids*
1897	One of the first orchid-growing societies is founded in Manchester, England

1903	Frenchman Noel Bernard successfully isolates the mycorrhizal fungi of certain orchids
1903	British musical comedy *The Orchid* premieres
1907	The moth *Xanthopan morganii* subspecies *praedicta*, with a 30-centimetre (12 in.) proboscis, is identified in Madagascar; it is capable of pollinating the unusual orchid *Angraecum sesquipedale*. The name *praedicta* references the fact that Darwin had, nearly fifty years earlier, predicted that such a moth would one day be found
1915	The second 'skull orchid' is put on display at New York's flower show
1916	Maurice-Alexandre Pouyanne first describes (in French) how insects attempt to mate with orchid flowers as a result of sexual deception
1921	The American Orchid Society is founded
1922	American plant physiologist Lewis Knudson discovers a way to germinate orchid seeds without the need of mycorrhizal fungi
1927	Edith Coleman, an Australian schoolteacher and naturalist, begins her studies of orchid sexual deception in Australian orchids
1928	The first species of an Australian underground orchid, *Rhizanthella gardneri*, known as the western underground orchid, is discovered
1930s	Walter Winchell, an American newspaper columnist and radio commentator, popularizes the expression 'orchids and scallions'
1931	John Collier's short story 'Green Thoughts' is published
1934	Author Rex Stout publishes his first Nero Wolfe story. Between 1934 and 1975, Stout will publish over thirty novels and numerous short stories and novellas about this fictional detective and orchid enthusiast
1935	Australian Tarlton Rayment, in his book *A Cluster of Bees*, first uses the term 'pseudocopulation' to describe sexual deception in orchids

1937	Oakes Ames publishes his paper 'Pollination of Orchids through Pseudocopulation'
1940	American newspaper comic strip series *Brenda Starr, Reporter* is created by female cartoonist Dale Messick. Starr's love interest is a mysterious character who repeatedly sends her black orchids. The series concluded after seventy years in 2011
1943	The first iteration of the Black Orchid superhero, starring Judy Allen, is published in comic book form
1970s	DC publishes an updated version of the superhero Black Orchid in an ongoing comic book series
1973	The CITES (Convention on International Trade in Endangered Species of Wild Fauna and Flora) international treaty is created
1979	James Bond film *Moonraker* is released. Its villain, Hugo Drax, threatens to destroy humanity with his evil plan, 'Operation Orchid', which will use a toxic chemical derived from the (fictional) orchid species *Orchidae nigra*
1982	Broadcast of 'Black Orchid', a two-part episode of British television series *Doctor Who*. Set in 1920s England, it features an agitated and murderous orchid collector and botanist who discovered a rare black orchid
1989	Vertigo Comics publishes a new *Black Orchid* superhero narrative, written by Neil Gaiman and illustrated by Dave McKean
1998	Susan Orlean's non-fiction book *The Orchid Thief* is published and becomes a best-seller
2002	The film *Adaptation*, written by Charlie Kaufman, directed by Spike Jonze and starring Nicolas Cage and Meryl Streep, is released. It is an 'adaptation' of Orlean's *The Orchid Thief*
2005	An extinct bee, with orchid pollinia of *Mellorchis caribea* attached, is found encased in amber in the Dominican Republic. It is dated as being 15–20 million years old
2016	The most recent species of Australian underground orchid, *Rhizanthella speciosa*, is discovered

References
❧

Introduction

1 David Attenborough, 'Foreword', in *Orchid Conservation*, ed. Kingsley W. Dixon et al. (Borneo, 2003), p. xi.

1 Understanding Orchids

1 *Xerophilia*, Special Issue no. 3 (January 2014).
2 Dan Torre, *Cactus* (London, 2017), pp. 24–5.
3 Hua Deng et al., 'Evolutionary History of PEPC Genes in Green Plants: Implications for the Evolution of CAM in Orchids', *Molecular Phylogenetics and Evolution*, XCIV (2016), pp. 559–64.
4 Gerhard Zotz and U. Winkler, 'Aerial Roots of Epiphytic Orchids: The Velamen Radicum and Its Role in Water and Nutrient Uptake', *Oecologia*, CLXXI/3 (March 2013), pp. 733–41.
5 Anne Ronse, *Orchid: The Fatal Attraction* (Oostkamp, 2008), p. 72.
6 Joel L. Schiff, *Rare and Exotic Orchids: Their Nature and Cultural Significance* (Cham, 2018), p. 33.
7 David L. Jones, *A Complete Guide to Native Orchids of Australia* (Sydney, 2006), p. 14.
8 Stefania Sut et al., 'Bioactive Secondary Metabolites from Orchids (Orchidaceae)', *Chemistry and Biodiversity*, 14 (2017), p. 2.
9 Tim Wing Yam and Joseph Arditti, 'History of Orchid Propagation: A Mirror of the History of Biotechnology', *Plant Biotechnology Reports*, 3 (2009), pp. 1–56.
10 Ken Cameron, *Vanilla Orchids: Natural History and Cultivation* (Portland, OR, 2011), p. 38.
11 Yam and Arditti, 'History of Orchid Propagation'.
12 Lakshman Chandra De et al., *Commercial Orchids* (Berlin, 2014), p. 122.
13 Yam and Arditti, 'History of Orchid Propagation'.
14 Ibid.
15 Sut et al., 'Bioactive Secondary Metabolites', p. 2.

16 Yam and Arditti, 'History of Orchid Propagation'.
17 Charles Darwin, *The Various Contrivances by Which Orchids Are Fertilised by Insects* (London, 1877), p. 279.
18 Eng Soon Toh, *Medicinal Orchids of Asia* (Cham, 2016), p. 15.
19 Paul Bayman et al., 'Root Cause: Mycorrhizal Fungi of Vanilla and Prospects for Biological Control of Root Rots', in *Handbook of Vanilla Science and Technology*, ed. Daphna Havkin-Frenkel and Faith C. Belanger (Hoboken, NJ, 2018).
20 Thomas J. Givnish et al., 'Orchid Historical Biogeography, Diversification, Antarctica and the Paradox of Orchid Dispersal', *Journal of Biogeography*, XLIII (2016), pp. 1905–16.
21 Santiago R. Ramirez et al., 'Dating the Origin of the Orchidaceae from a Fossil Orchid with Its Pollinator', *Nature*, CDXLVIII/30 (August 2007), p. 1042.
22 Sut et al., 'Bioactive Secondary Metabolites', p. 2.

2 The Secret Life of Orchids

1 Retha Edens-Meier and Peter Bernhardt, 'Summary', in *Darwin's Orchids: Then and Now*, ed. Retha Edens-Meier and Peter Bernhardt (Chicago, IL, 2014), p. 330.
2 S. D. Johnson and T. J. Edwards, 'The Structure and Function of Orchid Pollinaria', *Plant Systematics and Evolution*, CCXXII (2000), pp. 243–69.
3 Sandra Knapp, *Extraordinary Orchids* (London, 2021), p. 94.
4 David W. Roubik, 'Orchids and Neotropical Pollinators since Darwin's Time', in *Darwin's Orchids*, ed. Edens-Meier and Bernhardt, p. 233.
5 Knapp, *Extraordinary Orchids*, p. 76.
6 Robert A. Raguso and Andre Kessler, 'Speaking in Chemical Tongues: Decoding the Language of Plant Volatiles', in *The Language of Plants: Science, Philosophy, Literature*, ed. Monica Gagliano et al. (Minneapolis, MN, and London, 2017), p. 34.
7 Richard J. Waterman and Martin I. Bidartondo, 'Deception Above, Deception Below: Linking Pollination and Mycorrhizal Biology of Orchids', *Journal of Experimental Botany*, LIX/5 (2008), pp. 1085–96.
8 Jana Jersáková et al., 'Mechanisms and Evolution of Deceptive Pollination in Orchids', *Biology Review*, LXXXI (2006), pp. 219–35.
9 Waterman and Bidartondo, 'Deception Above, Deception Below'.
10 Raguso and Kessler, 'Speaking in Chemical Tongues', pp. 34–6.
11 Jersáková et al., 'Mechanisms and Evolution', pp. 219–35.
12 Anne Ronse, *Orchid: TheFatal Attraction* (Oostkamp, 2008), p. 133.
13 Jennifer Brodmann et al., 'Orchid Mimics Honey Bee Alarm Pheromone in Order to Attract Hornets for Pollination', *Current Biology*, XIX (25 August 2009), pp. 1368–72.
14 Raguso and Kessler, 'Speaking in Chemical Tongues', p. 36.
15 Ronse, *Orchid*, p. 86.
16 Jersáková et al., 'Mechanisms and Evolution', pp. 219–35.

17 Ibid.
18 Knapp, *Extraordinary Orchids*, p. 93.
19 Jersáková et al., 'Mechanisms and Evolution', pp. 219–23.
20 Mark Chase et al., *The Book of Orchids* (Brighton, 2017), p. 230.
21 Nicolas J. Vereecken, 'Deceptive Behavior in Plants: 1. Pollination by Sexual Deception in Orchids: A Host–Parasite Perspective', in *Plant–Environment Interactions: From Sensory Plant Biology to Active Plant Behavior*, ed. František Baluška (Berlin, 2009), p. 213.
22 Edens-Meier and Bernhardt, 'Summary', p. 331.
23 Jersáková et al., 'Mechanisms and Evolution', pp. 219–35.
24 Vereecken, 'Deceptive Behavior in Plants', p. 207.
25 Ibid.
26 Raguso and Kessler, 'Speaking in Chemical Tongues', pp. 34–6.
27 Ibid.
28 Edens-Meier and Bernhardt, 'Summary', p. 332.
29 Monica Gagliano, 'Breaking the Silence: Green Mudras and the Faculty of Language in Plants', in *The Language of Plants*, ed. Gagliano et al., pp. 91–2.
30 Ibid.
31 Jeremy Campbell, *The Liar's Tale: A History of Falsehood* (New York, 2001), p. 18.
32 Waterman and Bidartondo, 'Deception Above, Deception Below', p. 1090.
33 Dan Torre, *Carnivorous Plants* (London, 2019).
34 Chase et al., *Book of Orchids*, p. 54.
35 '*Aracamunia liesneri*', www.orchidspecies.com, accessed 10 November 2021.
36 Knapp, *Extraordinary Orchids*, p. 88.
37 Hanne N. Rasmussen and Dennis F. Whigham, 'The Underground Phase: A Special Challenge in Studies of Terrestrial Orchid Populations', *Botanical Journal of the Linnean Society*, CXXVI (1998), pp. 49–64.
38 Jeremy Bougoure et al,, 'Habitat Characteristics of the Rare Underground Orchid *Rhizanthella gardneri*', *Australian Journal of Botany*, LVI (2008), pp. 501–11.
39 Mark A. Clements and David L. Jones, 'Notes on Australasian Orchids 6: A New Species of *Rhizanthella* (Diurideae, Subtribe Prasophyllinae) from Eastern Australia', *Lankesteriana*, XX/2 (2020), pp. 221–7.
40 V. Rico-Gray and P. S. Oliveira, *The Ecology and Evolution of Ant–Plant Interactions* (Chicago, IL, 2007), p. 90.
41 Ibid., p. 167.
42 Ibid., p. 168.
43 Henry Ogg Forbes, *A Naturalist's Wanderings in the Eastern Archipelago from 1878 to 1883* [1885], quoted in Philip Short, *In Pursuit of Plants* (Crawley, Western Australia, 2003), p. 101.

3 Discovering Orchids

1 Eng Soon Teoh, *Orchids as Aphrodisiac, Medicine or Food* (Cham, 2019), p. 1.
2 Lewis Castle, *Orchids: Their Structure, History and Culture* (London 1886), p. 40.
3 Ibid.

4 J. Dybowski, 'The Rare Forms of Orchids', *Decorator and Furnisher*, XV/5 (1890), pp. 141–2.
5 Peter Bernhardt and Retha Edens-Meier, 'Darwin's Orchids (1862, 1877): Origins, Development, and Impact', in *Darwin's Orchids: Then and Now*, ed. Retha Edens-Meier and Peter Bernhardt (Chicago, IL, 2014), p 5
6 Dybowski, 'Rare Forms of Orchids', pp. 141–2.
7 Florence Thinard, *Explorers' Botanical Notebook* (New York, 2016), p. 122.
8 Sue Shephard and Toby Musgrave, *Blue Orchid and Big Tree: Plant Hunters William and Thomas Lobb and the Victorian Mania for the Exotic* (Bristol, 2014), p. 115.
9 Frederick Boyle, *About Orchids – a Chat* (London, 1893), pp. 26–8.
10 Joel L. Schiff, *Rare and Exotic Orchids: Their Nature and Cultural Significance* (Cham, 2018), p. 16.
11 George Ure Skinner, quoted in Philip Short, *In Pursuit of Plants* (Crawley, Western Australia, 2003), p. 263.
12 Albert Millican, *Travels and Adventures of an Orchid Hunter* (London, 1891), pp. 149–51.
13 Ibid., p. 158.
14 Thinard, *Explorers' Botanical Notebook*, p. 122.
15 Boyle, *About Orchids*, p. 29.
16 Frederick Boyle, *The Woodlands Orchids – Described and Illustrated with Stories of Orchid-Collecting* (London, 1901), p. 120.
17 Boyle, *About Orchids*, p. 31.
18 *Wood County Reporter*, Grand Rapids, WI (18 March 1915).
19 Paul Wood, *Orchid Isles: The Story of Orchids in Hawai'i* (Waipahu, HI, 2006), p. 52.
20 Michael Leapman, *The Ingenious Mr Fairchild: The Forgotten Father of the Flower Garden* (London, 2000), p. 245.
21 John Saul, *A Descriptive Catalogue of Orchids for 1882* (Washington, DC, 1882).
22 Edward Gillett, *Southwick Nurseries – Wholesale Trade List* (Southwick, MA, 1907).
23 David Lee, *Nature's Palette: The Science of Plant Color* (Chicago, IL, 2007), p. 166.
24 Mr H. J. Veitch, 'The Hybridisation of Orchid', *Report on the Orchid Conference, South Kensington, May 12th and 13th, 1885* (London, 1886), p. 47.
25 *Price List of Orchids, Lager & Hurrell Orchid Growers and Importers* (Summit, NJ, 1900).
26 *Pitcher and Manda Plant Catalogue* (1892).
27 *Catalogue of Cypripediums – The United States Nurseries* (Short Hills, NJ, 1889).
28 *The Christian Union*, XVII/4 (23 January 1878), p. 86.
29 James Agee, 'The U.S. Commercial Orchid', *Fortune* (December 1935).
30 Ibid., p. 659.
31 Ibid., p. 672.
32 Ibid., p. 667.
33 Ibid., p. 672.
34 Ibid.
35 Robert Kift, *The Retail Flower Shop* (New York, 1930), p. 168.

36 Wood, *Orchid Isles*, p. 47.
37 Lakshman Chandra De et al., *Commercial Orchids* (Berlin, 2014).
38 Shephard and Musgrave, *Blue Orchid and Big Tree*, p. 114.
39 Bernhardt and Edens-Meier, 'Darwin's Orchids (1862, 1877)', p. 11.
40 Charles Darwin, *The Various Contrivances by Which Orchids Are Fertilised by Insects* (London, 1877), p. 179.
41 Ibid.
42 Ibid., p. 88.
43 Ibid., p. 163.
44 Jana Jersáková et al., 'Mechanisms and Evolution of Deceptive Pollination in Orchids', *Biological Reviews*, 81 (2006), pp. 219–35.
45 Darwin, *Various Contrivances*, p. 37.
46 Ibid.
47 Danielle Clode, *The Wasp and the Orchid: The Remarkable Life of Australian Naturalist Edith Coleman* (Sydney, 2018), p. 182.
48 Ibid.
49 Ibid.
50 Ibid., p. 186.
51 Ibid., p. 193.
52 Gilles Deleuze and Félix Guattari, *A Thousand Plateaus: Capitalism and Schizophrenia* (Minneapolis, MN, 1987), p. 11.
53 Ibid., p. 293.

4 Picturing Orchids

1 Martin Hůla and Jaroslav Flegr, 'What Flowers Do We Like? The Influence of Shape and Color on the Rating of Flower Beauty', *PeerJ*, IV (2016), pp. 1–29.
2 George Hansen, *The Orchid Hybrids: Enumeration and Classification of All Hybrids of Orchids Published up to October 15, 1895* (London, 1895), p. 49.
3 Ibid.
4 M. C. Cooke, *Freaks and Marvels of Plant Life, or Curiosities of Vegetation* (London, 1881), p. 268.
5 C. M. Tracy, 'The Orchids', *American Naturalist*, II/7 (September 1868), pp. 342–51.
6 Cooke, *Freaks and Marvels*, p. 429.
7 James Bateman, *The Orchidaceae of Mexico and Guatemala* (London, 1843).
8 Ibid.
9 A. Kumbaric et al., 'Orchids in the Roman Culture and Iconography: Evidence for the First Representations in Antiquity', *Journal of Cultural Heritage*, XIV (2013), pp. 311–16.
10 Ibid.
11 Ibid.
12 Louis Liger, *The Compleat Florist* (London, 1706), p. 269. Also quoted in Jim Endersby, *Orchid: A Cultural History* (Chicago, IL, 2016), p. 59.
13 Endersby, *Orchid*, pp. 59–61.

14 Kumbaric et al., 'Orchids in the Roman Culture'.
15 Richard Folkard, *Plant-Lore, Legends and Lyrics* (London, 1892), p. 541.
16 Lawrence J. Crockett, 'The Identification of a Plant in the Unicorn Tapestries', *Metropolitan Museum Journal*, XVII (1982), pp. 15–22.
17 *Hamlet* (c 1599), Act IV, scene vii, ll. 169–72.
18 J H. Ingram, *Flora Symbolica* (London, 1868), p. 359.
19 Monica Merlin, 'The Nanjing Courtesan Ma Shouzhen (1548–1604): Gender, Space and Painting in the Late Ming Pleasure Quarter', in *Gender and the City before Modernity*, ed. L. Foxhall and G. Neher (Oxford, 2012), pp. 140–62.
20 Sungsook Hong Setton, 'Tao of Orchid', www.sungsooksetton.com, accessed 3 March 2021.
21 Fang Zong, 'Four Noble Plants in Chinese Culture Part 2: Orchid', https://storiesfromthemuseumfloor.wordpress.com, accessed 3 March 2021.
22 Ma Shouzhen, *Orchid and Rock*, www.metmuseum.org, accessed 3 March 2021.
23 Setton, 'Tao of Orchid'.
24 Merlin, 'Nanjing Courtesan', p. 152.
25 Thanh Huynh, 'From Mei Lanfang to Li Yugang: Theorizing Female-Impersonating Aesthetics in Post-1976 China', *International Communication of Chinese Culture*, VII/3 (2020), pp. 259–91.
26 Jess Zhang, 'Orchid Flower Fingers', https://journeys.dartmouth.edu/folklorearchive, accessed 6 October 2021.
27 John Gerard, *Generall Historie of Plantes* (London, 1597).
28 Ernst Haeckel, *The Riddle of the Universe at the Close of the Nineteenth Century*, trans. Joseph McCabe (London, 1901), p. 181.
29 Harvard Museum of Natural History, https://hmnh.harvard.edu/glass-flowers, accessed 11 October 2021.
30 Clare Phillips, ed., *Bejewelled by Tiffany: 1837–1987* (New Haven, CT, 2006).
31 Ibid.
32 *Tiffany & Co. Paris Exposition Catalogue* (New York, 1889).
33 *Tiffany & Co. Blue Book* (New York, 1894).
34 Karen E. Quinn, 'A Rare Beauty: The Orchid in Western Art', in *Orchid Biology: Reviews and Perspectives*, ed. Tiiu Kull, Joseph Arditti and Sek Man Wong (Berlin, 2009), vol. X, pp. 223–4.
35 Narin Hassan, '"A Perfect World of Wonders": Marianne North and the Pleasures and Pursuits of Botany', in *Strange Science: Investigating the Limits of Knowledge in the Victorian Age*, ed. Lara Pauline Karpenko and Shalyn Rae Claggett (Ann Arbor, MI, 2016), p. 71.
36 Georgia O'Keeffe, *Narcissa's Last Orchid*, https://artmuseum.princeton.edu, accessed 30 August 2021.
37 Arthur Chadwick, 'Orchids: Georgia O'Keeffe Orchid Paintings', *Richmond Times-Dispatch*, https://richmond.com, 9 November 2019.
38 Georgia O'Keeffe, quoted in Carol Gracie, *Florapedia: A Brief Compendium of Floral Lore* (Princeton, NJ, 2021), p. 96.
39 Gina la Morte, 'Earth's Gold', *Boho*, X (Spring 2011), p. 28.

40 See www.madelinevonfoerster.com, accessed 1 February 2021.

41 Madeline von Foerster, 'Orchid Cabinet' (2018), ibid.

42 'Madeline von Foerster', *Miroir Magazine* (October 2019), p. 102.

43 Debora Moore, 'Artist Statement', www.deboramoore.com, accessed 16 October 2021.

44 Ibid.

45 Ibid.

46 Laura Bradley, 'Marc Quinn on Orchids', *AnOther*, www.anothermag.com, accessed 7 October 2021.

47 Ibid.

5 Pop Culture Orchids

1 Brian Williams, *Orchids for Everyone* (London, 1980), p. 12.

2 Charles Darwin, *The Power of Movement in Plants* (London, 1880), p. 576.

3 Anne Pratt, *The Flowering Plants of Great Britain* (London, 1855), p. 188.

4 J. G. Hunt, 'Natural History Studies', *Friends' Intelligencer*, XXXIX/1 (1882), p. 10, quoted in Tina Gianquitto, 'Criminal Botany Progress, Degeneration, and Darwin's Insectivorous Plants', in *America's Darwin: Darwinian Theory and U.S. Literary Culture*, ed. Tina Gianquitto and Lydia Fisher (Athens, GA, 2014), p. 235.

5 Cesare Lombroso, *Criminal Man* (1884), ed. and trans. M. Gibson and N. H. Rafter (Durham, NC, 2006), p. 167. Also quoted in Dawn Keetley, 'Introduction: Six Theses on Plant Horror; or, Why Are Plants Horrifying?', in *Plant Horror: Approaches to the Monstrous Vegetal in Fiction and Film*, ed. Dawn Keetley and Angela Tenga (London, 2016), p. 17.

6 Alfred Russel Wallace, 'The Colors of Animals and Plants', *American Naturalist*, XI/11 (November 1877), p. 650.

7 James Hingston, *The Australian Abroad – Branches from the Main Routes round The World* (London, 1879), pp. 199–200.

8 H. G. Wells, 'The Flowering of the Strange Orchid', in *The Stolen Bacillus and Other Incidents* (London, 1895), p. 18.

9 Ibid., p. 24.

10 Ibid., p. 23.

11 Ibid., p. 32.

12 Ibid., p. 35.

13 John Collier, 'Green Thoughts', *Harper's Magazine* (May 1931), pp. 691–701.

14 *Pokémon Super Extra Deluxe Essential Handbook* (Sydney, 2021).

15 Marjorie L. C. Pickthall, 'The Black Orchid', *McClure's Magazine*, XXXV/5 (September 1910), p. 568.

16 'Slaves of the Orchid Goddess', *Baffling Mysteries*, 14 (March 1953).

17 'Black Orchid', *All New Short Story Comics*, 2 (March 1943).

18 Albert and Florence Magarian, *The Black Orchid* (1944).

19 Sheldon Mayer, *Adventure Comics Presents Black Orchid*, XXXIX/429 (September–October 1973), p. 1.

20 Ibid., p. 3.

21 Ibid., p. 7.
22 Neil Gaiman and Dave McKean, *Black Orchid* (New York, 1991), p. 112.
23 Rex Stout, *Black Orchids* (New York, 1942), p. 8.
24 Ibid., p. 100.
25 Dale Messick, *Brenda Starr, Reporter*, 1 (October–December 1963), p. 8.
26 *Punch* (17 December 1902), p. 419.
27 Daniel Herbert, 'On This Day: "The Orchid Man" Georges Carpentier Passes Away at the Age of 81', *Boxing News Online*, www.boxingnewsonline. net, 28 October 2018.
28 Lore Perfumery, 'The Orchid Man', www.loreperfumery.com.au, accessed 8 October 2021.
29 Jack Banner, 'The Private Life of Walter Winchell', *Radio Guide*, IV/12 (1935), p. 28.

6 Consuming Orchids

1   Beth Gott, 'Ecology of Root Use by the Aborigines of Southern Australia in Archaeology in Oceania', *Plants and People*, XVII/1 (April 1982), pp. 59–67.
2   Bruce Pascoe, *Dark Emu: Aboriginal Australia and the Birth of Agriculture* (Broome, Western Australia, 2018), p. 22.
3   Tim Low, *Wild Food Plants of Australia* (Sydney, 1988), p. 134.
4   Ibid.
5   Quoted ibid., p. 196.
6   Le Griffon, quoted in Pascoe, *Dark Emu*, p. 23.
7   Bruce Munday, *Those Wild Rabbits: How They Shaped Australia* (Adelaide, 2017), p. 6.
8   Leonard J. Lawler, 'Ethnobotany of the Orchidaceae', in *Orchid Biology Reviews and Perspectives*, ed. Joseph Arditti (London, 1984), vol. III, pp. 27–149.
9   Theophrastus, quoted in Andrew Dalby, 'The Name of the Rose Again; or, What Happened to Theophrastus on Aphrodisiacs?', *Petits Propos Culinaires*, 64 (2000), pp. 9–15.
10 Nicholas Culpeper, *Culpeper's Complete Herbal* (London, 1814), p. 130.
11 Ibid.
12 H. S. Puri, *Rasayana: Ayurvedic Herbs for Longevity and Rejuvenation* (London, 2003), p. 244.
13 Lewis Castle, *Orchids: Their Structure, History and Culture* (London, 1886).
14 Quoted in Layinka Swinburne, 'Dancing with the Mermaids: Ship's Biscuit and Portable Soup', in *Food on The Move: Proceedings of The Oxford Symposium on Food and Cookery 1996*, ed. Harlan Walker (Totnes, 1997), p. 316.
15 *Encyclopaedia Londinensis* (London, 1820), p. 705.
16 J. Moult, 'A Letter from Mr. J. Moult to Dr. Percival, of Manchester, F.R.S. Containing a New Manner of Preparing Salep', *Philosophical Transactions*, LIX (1769), pp. 1–3.
17 Ibid.
18 Elizabeth Hammond, *Modern Domestic Cookery* (London, 1816), p. 197.

19 Mrs Smith, *The Female Economist* (London, 1819), p. 148.

20 Friedrich A. Flückiger and Daniel Hanbury, *Pharmacographia: A History of the Principal Drugs of Vegetable Origin, Met with in Great Britain and British India* (London, 1879), p. 656.

21 *The Slang Dictionary: Etymological, Historical and Anecdotal* (London, 1913), p. 275.

22 Holly Chase, 'Suspect Salep', in *Look and Feel – Studies in Texture, Appearance and Incidental Characteristics of Food: Proceedings of the Oxford Symposium on Food and Cookery, 1993*, ed. Harlan Walker (Totnes, 1994), p. 45.

23 A. Davidson, *Oxford Companion to Food* (London, 2006), p. 2489.

24 Flückiger and Hanbury, *Pharmacographia*, p. 656.

25 Anna Kreziou et al., 'Harvesting of Salep Orchids in North-Western Greece Continues to Threaten Natural Populations', *Oryx*, L/3 (2016), pp. 393–6.

26 Ibid.

27 Holly Chase, 'Suspect Salep', *Saratosa Soundings*, https://skiplombardi.org, accessed 21 December 2021.

28 Kreziou et al., 'Harvesting of Salep Orchids'.

29 Ambayeba Muimba-Kankolongo et al., 'Non-Wood Forest Products, Markets, and Trade', in *Forest Policy, Economics, and Markets in Zambia*, ed. Phillimon Ng'andwe et al. (London, 2015), p. 78.

30 Ibid.

31 John R. Jackson, 'Orchid Tea', in *The Technologist* (London, 1866), vol. VI, p. 486.

32 *Mackie Brothers' Practical Guide to Candy Making* (1905), p. 56.

33 Lawler, 'Ethnobotany of the Orchidaceae'.

34 Lakshman Chandra De et al., *Commercial Orchids* (Berlin, 2014), p. 160.

35 Ibid.

36 Kenneth M. Cameron, 'Vanilla Phylogeny and Classification', in *Handbook of Vanilla Science and Technology*, ed. Daphna Havkin-Frenkel and Faith C. Belanger (Hoboken, NJ, 2018).

37 Ibid.

38 Ibid.

39 Patricia Rain and Pesach Lubinsky, 'Vanilla Use in Colonial Mexico and Traditional Totonac Vanilla Farming', in *Vanilla*, ed. Eric Odoux and Michel Grisoni (Boca Raton, FL, 2010), p. 251.

40 E. Curti Diaz, 'Cultivo y beneficiado de la vainilla en México', in *Folleto ténico para productores. Organización Nacional de Vainílleros Indígenas. Papantla* (Veracruz, 1995), English translation quoted in Juan Hernández-Hernández, 'Mexican Vanilla Production', in *Handbook*, ed. Havkin-Frenkel and Belanger, p. 96.

41 Ken Cameron, *Vanilla Orchids: Natural History and Cultivation* (Portland, OR, 2011), p. 16.

42 Ibid., p. 19.

43 Paul Bayman et al., 'Root Cause: Mycorrhizal Fungi of Vanilla and Prospects for Biological Control of Root Rots', in *Handbook*, ed. Havkin-Frenkel and Belanger, p. 447.

44 Hernández-Hernández, 'Mexican Vanilla Production', p. 85.
45 Ibid., p. 86.
46 Ibid., p. 88.
47 Ibid.
48 Ibid., p. 89.
49 Ibid., p. 90.
50 Joseph Burnett Company, *About Vanilla* (Boston, MA, 1900), p. 3.
51 G. A. Burdock and G. Fenaroli, *Fenaroli's Handbook of Flavor Ingredients* (London, 2009), pp. 273–5.
52 Mollie Bloudoff-Indelicato, 'Beaver Butts Emit Goo Used for Vanilla Flavoring', *National Geographic*, www.nationalgeographic.com, 2 October 2013.
53 G. A. Burdock, 'Safety Assessment of Castoreum Extract as a Food Ingredient', *International Journal of Toxicology*, XXVI (2007), pp. 51–5.
54 Bloudoff-Indelicato, 'Beaver Butts Emit Goo'.
55 Daphna Havkin-Frenkel et al., 'A Comprehensive Study of Composition and Evaluation of Vanilla Extracts in U.S. Retail Stores', in *Handbook*, ed. Havkin-Frenkel and Belanger.
56 Felix Buccellato, 'Vanilla in Perfumery and Beverage Flavors', in *Handbook*, ed. Havkin-Frenkel and Belanger.
57 Luca Turin, *The Secret of Scent: Adventures in Perfume and the Science of Smell* (London, 2006), p. 37.
58 Cameron, *Vanilla Orchids*, p. 9.
59 Buccellato, 'Vanilla in Perfumery'.
60 Fang Zong, 'Four Noble Plants in Chinese Culture Part Two: Orchids', https://storiesfromthemuseumfloor.wordpress.com, accessed 10 October 2021.
61 Joel L. Schiff, *Rare and Exotic Orchids: Their Nature and Cultural Significance* (Cham, 2018), p. 103.
62 Eng Soon Teoh, *Orchids as Aphrodisiac, Medicine or Food* (Cham, 2019), p. 55.
63 Ibid., p. 69.
64 Ibid., pp. 91–2.
65 Eng Soon Teoh, *Medicinal Orchids of Asia* (Cham, 2016).
66 Teoh, *Orchids as Aphrodisiac*, pp. 91–2.
67 Michelle A. Nguyen and Gulden Camci-Unal, 'Unconventional Tissue Engineering Materials in Disguise', *Trends in Biotechnology*, XXXVIII/2 (February 2020), pp. 178–90.

7 Orchid Conservation

1 Benjamin Samuel Williams, *The Orchid-Grower's Manual*, 6th edn (London, 1895), p. 13.
2 Ibid.
3 J. Murray Cox, *A Cultural Table of Orchidaceous Plants* (Sydney, 1946), p. 371.

4 Phillip J. Cribb et al., 'Orchid Conservation: A Global Perspective',
in *Orchid Conservation*, ed. Phillip J. Cribb et al. (Kota Kinabalu, Malaysia,
2003), p. 5.

5 Amy Hinsley, *The Role of Online Platforms in the Illegal Orchid Trade from South
East Asia* (Geneva, 2018), pp. 1–18.

6 Michael F. Fay, 'Orchid Conservation: How Can We Meet the Challenges
in the Twenty-First Century?', *Botanical Studies*, LIX/16 (2018), pp. 1–6.

7 Hinsley, *Role of Online Platforms*.

8 Cribb et al., 'Orchid Conservation', p. 4.

9 Shawn Tay, Jie He and Tim Wing Yam. 'CAM Plasticity in Epiphytic
Tropical Orchid Species Responding to Environmental Stress', *Botanical
Studies*, LX/7 (2019), pp. 1–15.

10 Cribb et al., 'Orchid Conservation', p. 2.

11 Ibid., p. 10.

12 Yuan-Yuan Meng et al., 'Are Fungi from Adult Orchid Roots the Best
Symbionts at Germination? A Case Study', *Mycorrhiza*, XXIX (2019),
pp. 541–7.

13 Cribb et al., 'Orchid Conservation', p. 15.

14 James Bateman, quoted in Mr H. J. Veitch, 'The Hybridisation of
Orchid', *Report on the Orchid Conference, South Kensington, May 12th and 13th, 1885*
(London, 1886), p. 49.

15 Barney Greer, *The Astonishing Stanhopeas* (Sydney, 1998), p. 73.

16 Richard Mabey, *Weeds: How Vagabond Plants Gatecrashed Civilisation and Changed
the Way We Think about Nature* (London, 2010), pp. 195–6.

17 Donald Watts, *Dictionary of Plant Lore* (London, 2007), p. 128.

18 Mark Chase et al., *The Book of Orchids* (Brighton, 2017), p. 513.

19 Ibid., p. 87.

20 Ibid., p. 248.

21 Nicholas S. G. Williams and John W. Morgan, 'The Native Temperate
Grasslands of South-Eastern Australia', in *Land of Sweeping Plains: Managing
and Restoring the Native Grasslands of South-Eastern Australia*, ed. Nicholas S. G.
Williams et al. (Melbourne, 2015), p. 52.

22 Rhi Storer, 'Orchid Thought to Be Extinct in UK Found on Roof of
London Bank', *The Guardian*, www.theguardian.com, 17 June 2021.

23 Phoebe Weston, 'Giant Orchids Found Growing Wild in UK for
First Time', *The Guardian*, www.theguardian.com, 1 April 2022.

24 P. T. Seaton et al., 'Ex Situ Conservation of Orchids in a Warming
World', *Botanical Review*, LXXVI (2010), pp. 193–203.

25 Ibid.

26 Frederick Boyle, *About Orchids – a Chat* (London, 1893), p. 2.

Further Reading

Bernhardt, Peter, and Retha Edens-Meier, eds, *Darwin's Orchids: Then and Now* (Chicago, IL, 2014)

Cameron, Ken, *Vanilla Orchids: Natural History and Cultivation* (Portland, OR, 2011)

Clode, Danielle, *The Wasp and the Orchid: The Remarkable Life of Australian Naturalist Edith Coleman* (Sydney, 2018)

Darwin, Charles, *The Various Contrivances by Which Orchids Are Fertilised by Insects* (London, 1877)

Dixon, Kingsley W., et al., eds, *Orchid Conservation* (Borneo, 2003)

Endersby, Jim, *Orchid: A Cultural History* (Chicago, IL, 2016)

Knapp, Sandra, *Extraordinary Orchids* (London, 2021)

Ronse, Anne, *Orchid: The Fatal Attraction* (Oostkamp, 2008)

Schiff, Joel L., *Rare and Exotic Orchids: Their Nature and Cultural Significance* (Cham, 2018)

Teoh, Eng Soon, *Medicinal Orchids of Asia* (Cham, 2016)

Associations and Websites

꙳

Akatsuka Orchid Gardens, Hawai'i
https://akatsukaorchid.com

American Orchid Society
www.aos.org

Australian Network for Plant Conservation
www.anpc.asn.au/orchids

Australian Orchid Council
www.orchidsaustralia.com.au

Gothenburg Botanical Garden
www.botaniska.se

North American Orchid Conservation Center
www.northamericanorchidcenter.org

Orchid Conservation Alliance
www.orchidconservationalliance.org

Orchid Society of Great Britain
www.osgb.org.uk

Royal Botanic Gardens Kew
www.kew.org/kew-gardens/plants/orchids-collection

Royal Horticultural Society
www.rhs.org.uk

Singapore Botanic Gardens, the National Orchid Garden
www.nparks.gov.sg/sbg/our-gardens/tyersall-entrance/national-orchid-garden

Smithsonian Gardens
https://gardens.si.edu/collections/plants/orchids

Société Française d'Orchidophilie
https://sfo-asso.fr

Acknowledgements

Thanks to the many orchid growers and enthusiasts who have shared their knowledge. Thanks to Michael Leaman, Phoebe Colley, Susannah Jayes, Alex Wild, Attila Kapitany, Randall Robinson and Victor Aprozeanu. Thanks to Thomas for suggesting castoreum, Kathy for suggesting Brenda Starr, Lucy for her common sense, Lienors for reading it, and Vivienne for her green thumb.

Photo Acknowledgements

The author and publishers wish to express their thanks to the below sources of illustrative material and/or permission to reproduce it.

The American Magazine: p. 155; *Baffling Mysteries*: p. 150; *The Black Orchid*: p. 151; DC Comics: p. 152; Dell Comics: p. 159; Flickr: pp. 179 (hamad M), 185 (Mark's Postcards from Beloit); Madeline von Foerster: p. 130; Galerie Pels-Leusden AG, Zürich, Switzerland: p. 127; Metropolitan Museum of Art, New York: pp. 106–7 (Gift of John D. Rockefeller Jr, 1937); Debora Moore: p. 133; public domain: pp. 8, 12, 17, 18, 19, 20, 22, 25, 30, 36, 38, 41, 48, 55, 56, 62, 64, 67, 68, 70, 71, 72, 73, 75, 77, 79, 80, 82, 85, 88, 89, 93, 99, 100, 101, 109, 110, 111, 112 left, 113 left and right, 116, 117, 120, 122, 124, 136, 141, 164, 167, 168, 169, 170, 175, 176, 188, 193, 204, 205, 211, 214, 216, 219; *Shock* magazine: p. 143; Tiffany and Co.: pp. 118, 119; Dan Torre: pp. 9, 10, 14, 16, 21, 23, 28, 31, 32, 33, 39, 45, 52, 54, 94, 96, 112 right, 210, 218, 222, 223; Victoria & Albert Museum, London: p. 104; Wikimedia Commons: pp. 11 (Björn S./CC BY-SA 3.0 Unported), 24 (OpenCage/CC BY-SA 2.5), 27 left (Unknown/CC BY 2.0), 27 right (Geoff Derrin/CC BY-SA 4.0 International), 34 (Alejandro Bayer Tamayo from Armenia, Colombia/CC BY-SA 2.0), 43 (Ong Poh Teck, Forest Research Institute Malaysia/CC BY 2.0), 50 (Geoff Derrin/CC BY-SA 4.0 International), 58 top (Kiran Gopi/CC BY-SA 4.0 International), 58 bottom (Kilitz Photography/CC BY 2.0), 60 left (Jean and Fred Hort/CC BY-SA 2.0), 60 right (Etienne Delannoy/CC BY-SA 4.0 International), 86 (Julian Herzog/CC BY-SA 4.0 International), 125 (Christie's/Public Domain), 139 (Pavel Kirillov from St Petersburg, Russia/CC BY-SA 2.0), 162 (NC Orchid from North Carolina, USA/CC BY 2.0), 182 (Little T889/CC BY-SA 4.0 International), 183 (Jojona/CC BY-SA 3.0 Unported), 186 (H. Zell/CC BY-SA 3.0 Unported), 191 (Kgv88/CC BY-SA 3.0 Unported), 192 (Ekrem Canli/CC BY-SA 3.0 Unported), 196 (David Monniaux/CC BY-SA 3.0 Unported), 197 (U.S. Department of Agriculture/Public Domain), 200 (Michelle Naherny/CC BY-SA 4.0 International), 208 (Andrew Massyn/CC BY-SA 3.0 Unported), 212 (Auckland Museum/CC BY-SA 4.0 International).

Index

Page numbers in *italics* indicate illustrations